St. Catharines Ontario Book 2 in Colour Photos, Saving Our History One Photo at a Time

Photography
by Barbara Raué
2018

Series Name:
Cruising Ontario

Book 190: St. Catharines Book 2

Cover photo: Dalhousie Avenue, Page 39

Series Name: Cruising Ontario
Saving Our History One Photo at a Time
in colour photos

Books Available in Alphabetical Order:
Aberfoyle, Acton, Alton, Amherstburg, Ancaster, Arthur, Aylmer, Ayr, Bloomingdale, Brantford, Burlington, Caledon, Caledonia, Cambridge, Clifford, Conestogo, Delhi, Dorchester to Aylmer, Drayton, Drumbo, Dundas, Eden Mills, Elmira, Elora, Essex, Fergus, Guelph, Hagersville, Hamilton, Hanover, Harriston, Hespeler, Jarvis, Kingston, Kingsville, Kitchener, Linwood, Listowel, London, Lucknow, Mono, Mount Forest, Neustadt, New Hamburg, Niagara-on-the-Lake, Oakville, Orangeville, Orillia, Owen Sound, Palmerston, Peterborough, Petrolia, Port Elgin, Preston, Rockwood, Sarnia, Seaforth, Sheffield, Shelburne, Simcoe, Southampton, St. Jacobs, St. Marys, St. Thomas, Stoney Creek, Stratford, Thamesford, Tillsonburg, Waterdown, Waterford, Waterloo, Welland, Wellesley, Windsor, Wingham, Woodstock

Book 157: Brockville
Book 158: Merrickville
Book 159: Smiths Falls
Book 160: Portland, Newboro
Book 161: Westport & Area
Book 162: Perth
Book 163-166: Belleville
Book 167-168: Port Colborne
Book 169: Erin in Colour
Book 170: Goderich in Colour
Book 171: Sault Ste. Marie
Book 172: Lake Superior
Book 173-176: Thunder Bay
Book 177-179: Paris

Book 180: St. George
Book 182-183: Burford
Book 184: Mt Pleasant, Onondaga, Newport
Book 185-186: Grimsby
Book 187: Toronto in Colour
Book 188: Collingwood Colour
Book 189-193: St. Catharines

Other Books by Barbara Raue

Coins of Gold

Arrows, Indians and Love

The Life and Times of Barbara
Volume 1: Inventions That Have Enhanced My Life
Volume 2: Entertainment That I Have Enjoyed
Volume 3: East Coast Trips
Volume 4: Olympics Have Always Intrigued Me
Volume 5: Wonders of the World
Volume 6: Caribbean Cruises We Have Enjoyed
Volume 7: Animals
Volume 8: Storms and Other Major Disasters in My Lifetime
Volume 9: Wars, Terrorist Attacks and Major Disasters

The Cromwell Family Book

Laura Secord Discovered

Daddy Where Are You?

Montana Series
Book 1: Montana Dream
Book 2: Life on the Montana Frontier
Book 3: Montana to Boston and Back
Book 4: Montana Sons Go to War
Book 5: Montana Sons Return From War

Visit Barbara's website to view all of her books
http://barbararaue.ca

Table of Contents

Dalhousie Avenue — Page 6

Elgin Street — Page 45

Ann Street — Page 50

Brock Street — Page 54

Simcoe Street — Page 59

Lakeport Road – carousel — Page 63

Architectural Terms — Page 66

Building Styles — Page 68

Port Dalhousie is a community in St. Catharines known for its waterfront appeal. It is historically significant as the terminus for the first three (19th century) routes of the Welland Canal, built in 1820, 1845 and 1889. The city's most popular beach, on the shore of Lake Ontario, is located in Port Dalhousie at Lakeside Park. The park is home to an antique carousel which was carved by Charles I. D. Looff in 1905 and brought to St. Catharines in 1921. It continues to provide amusement for young and old alike, at just 5 cents a ride. Port Dalhousie is named for George Ramsay, 9th Earl of Dalhousie, Governor General of British North America from 1820-1828.

At the time of European colonization, the British Crown appropriated the land from the Neutral Indians, and transferred title of the area to Captain Peter Tenbroeck, a United Empire Loyalist officer in Butler's Rangers, as part of an 800 acre land grant. Tenbroeck and other settlers established farms along the Twelve Mile Creek. Within a few years, ships began to ply the waters of Lake Ontario, but only small craft could navigate to the fledgling mills and hamlet of Shipman's Corners, later St. Catharines.

The northern entrance to the Welland Canal was at Port Dalhousie. Industries and services to meet the needs of the growing settlement were established. In 1837, a Scottish boat builder called Robert Abbey started a shipyard at Port Dalhousie, building yawls, sailing yachts and eventually steam yachts.

Confederation in 1867 was a major factor in the building of the Third Welland Canal. A new and enlarged waterway was needed for the larger steamers on the Great Lakes. By 1890 almost 300,000 tons of cargo were shipped along the canal each year, primarily wheat, corn, coal and forest products. By 1914, this had increased to almost four million tons. Further canal enlargements were demanded and a new Welland Ship Canal was completed in 1930 which bypassed Port Dalhousie.

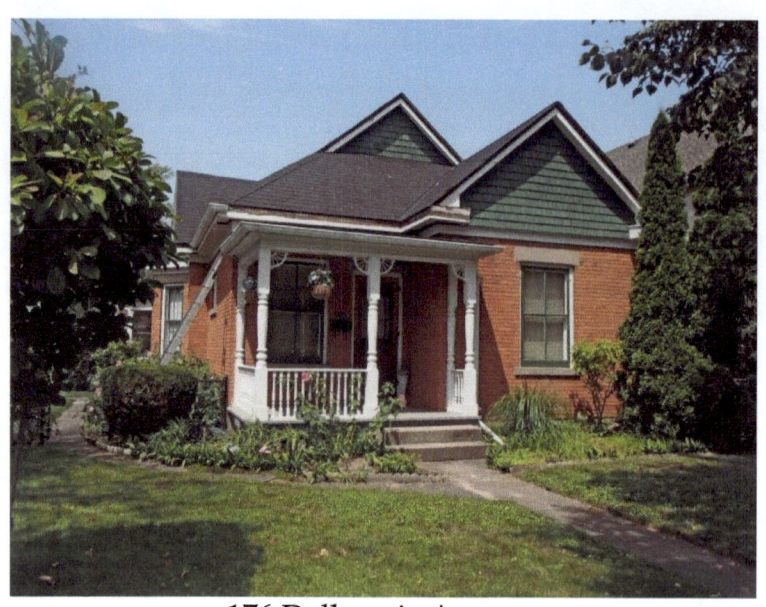

176 Dalhousie Avenue

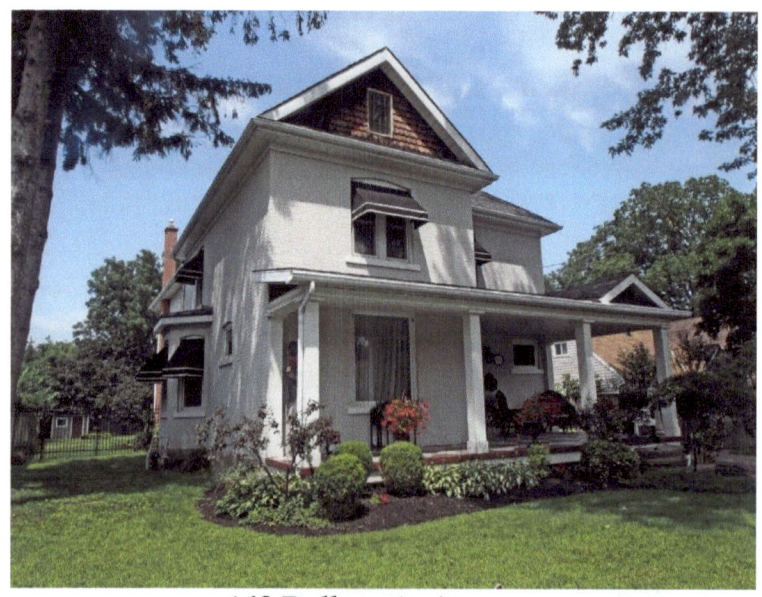

168 Dalhousie Avenue

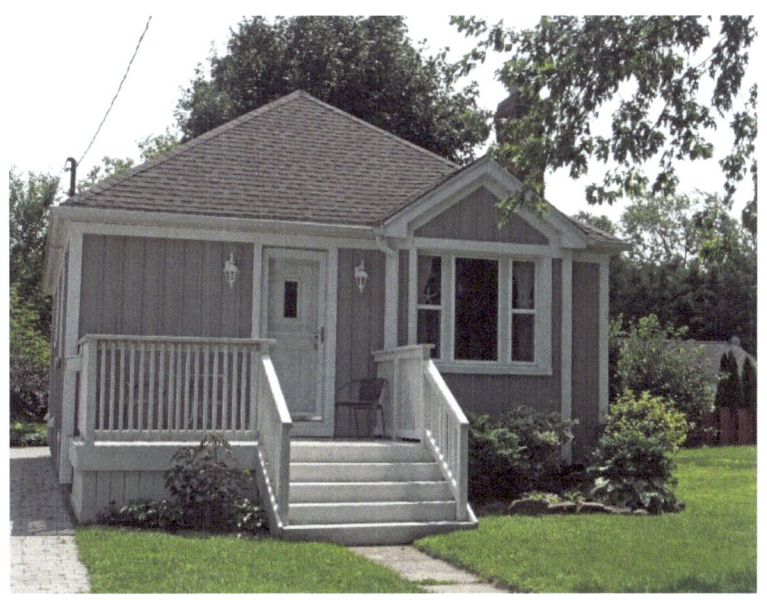

Dalhousie Avenue – Regency Cottage

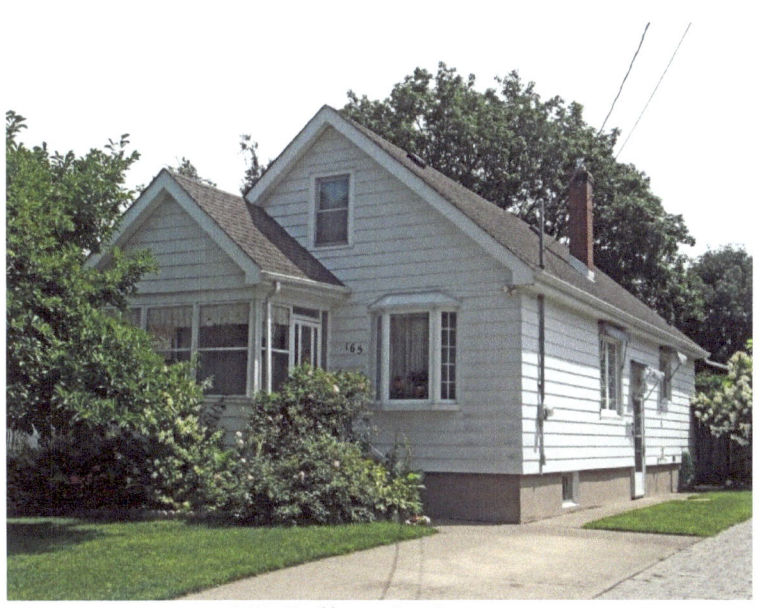

165 Dalhousie Avenue

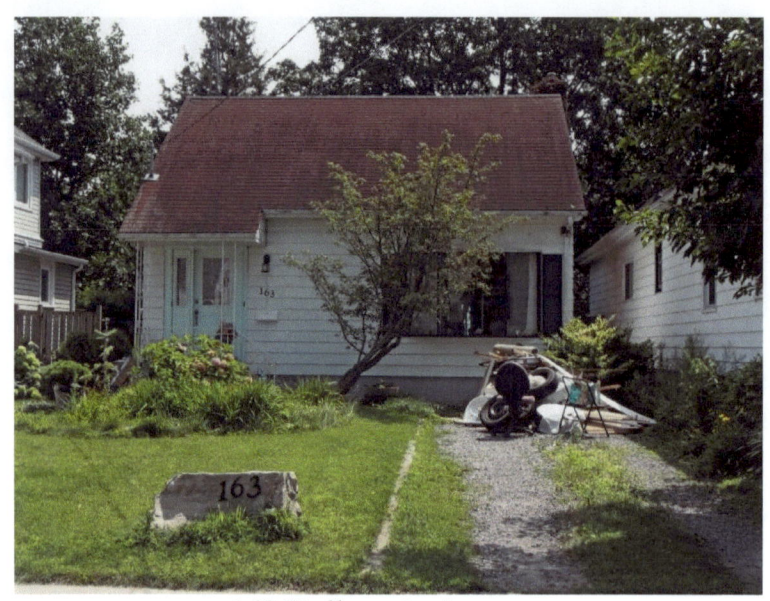

163 Dalhousie Avenue

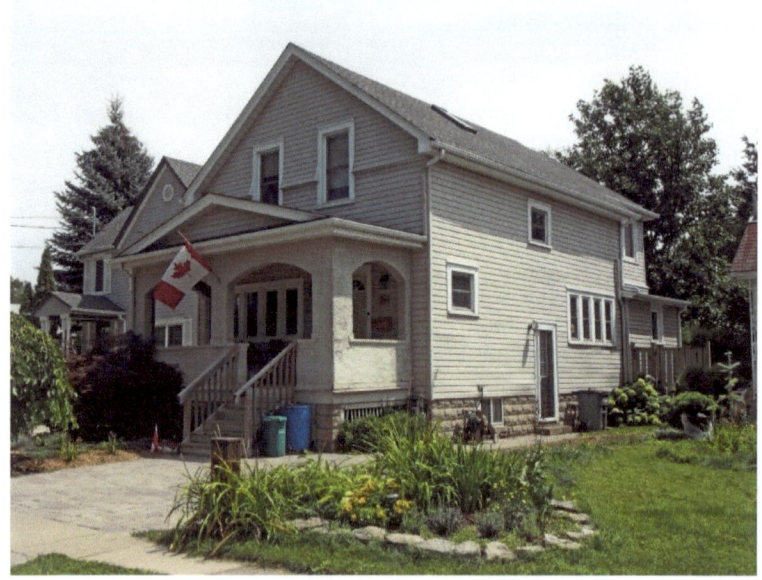

Dalhousie Avenue - pediment

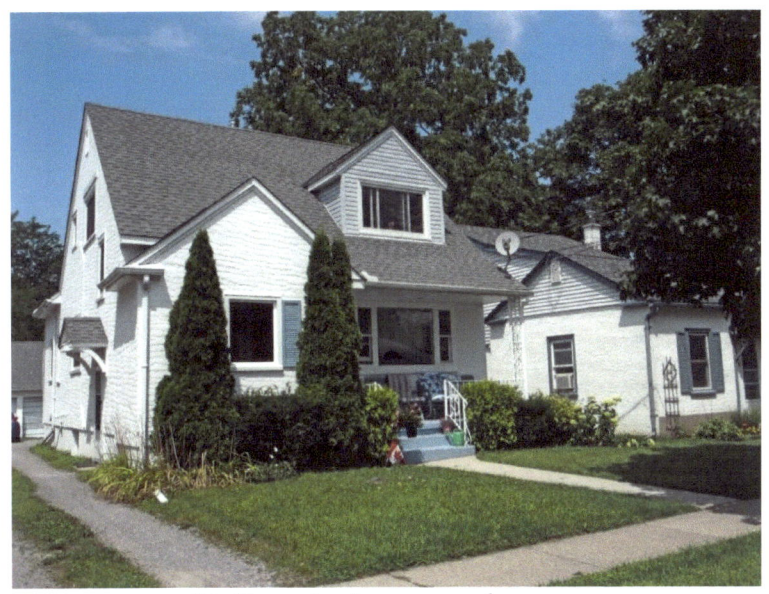

Dalhousie Avenue - dormer

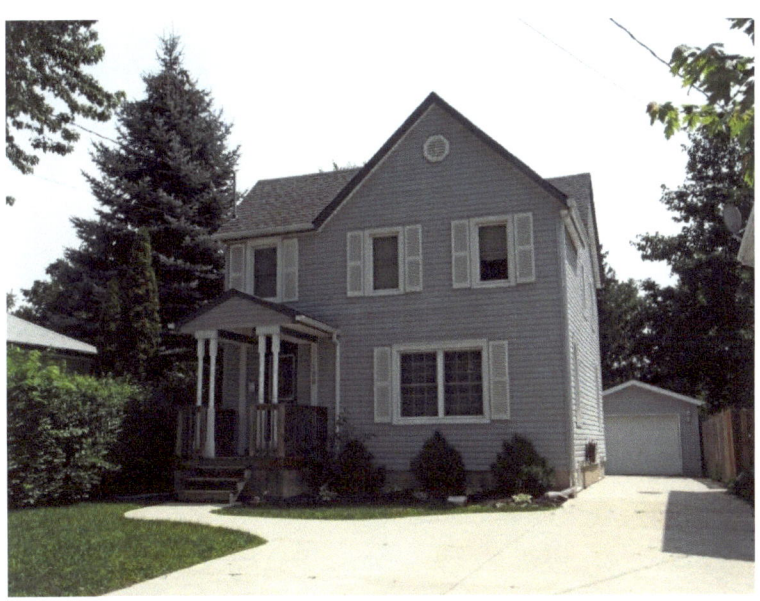

159 Dalhousie Avenue

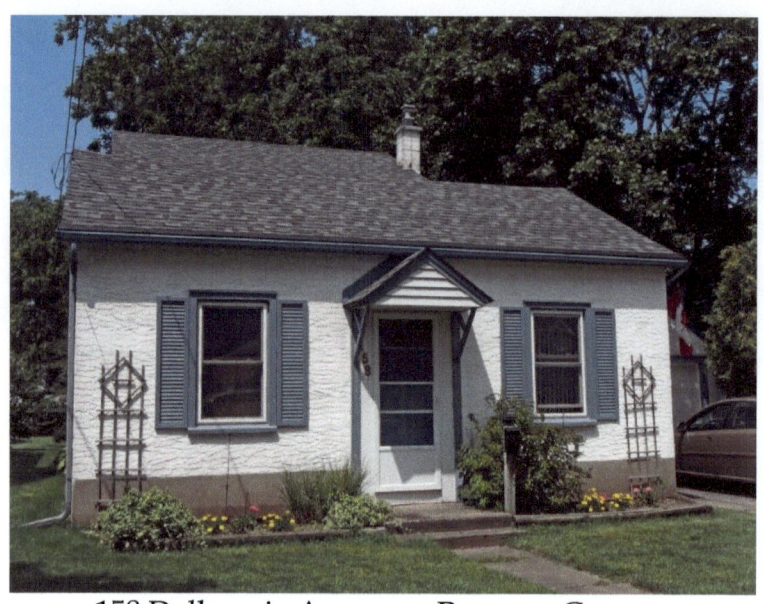

158 Dalhousie Avenue – Regency Cottage

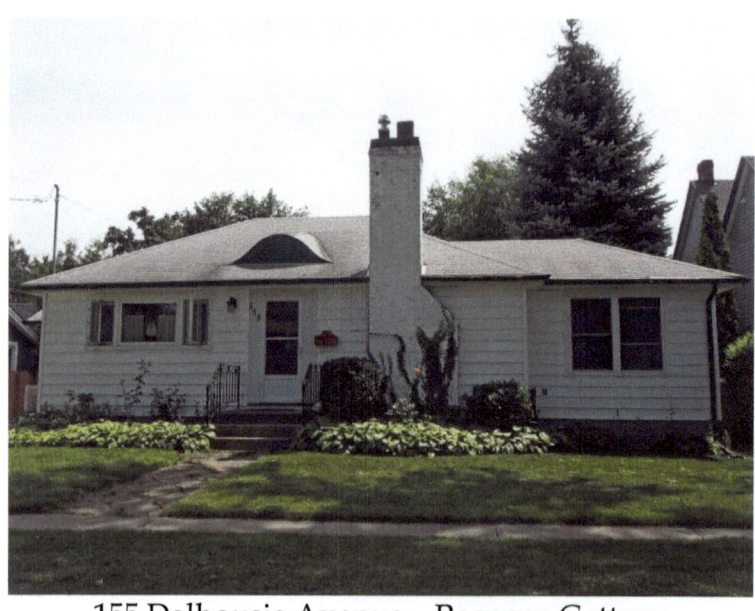

155 Dalhousie Avenue – Regency Cottage

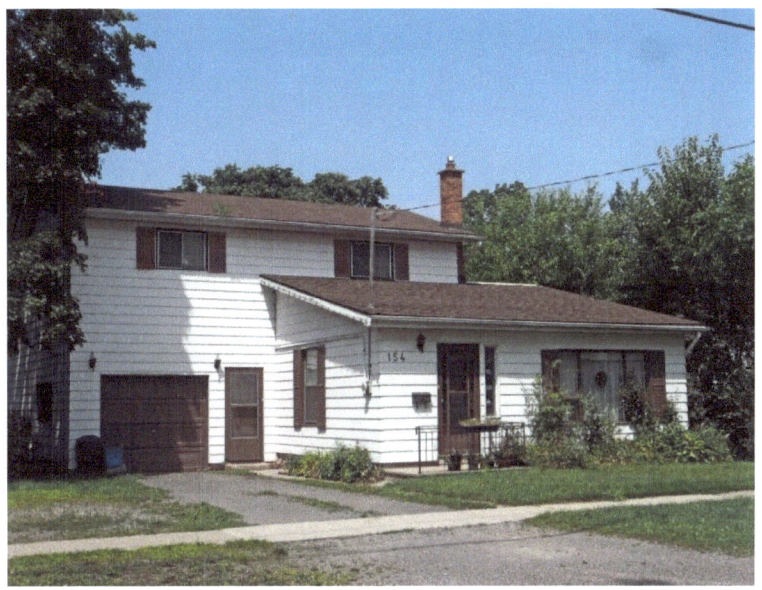

154 Dalhousie Avenue

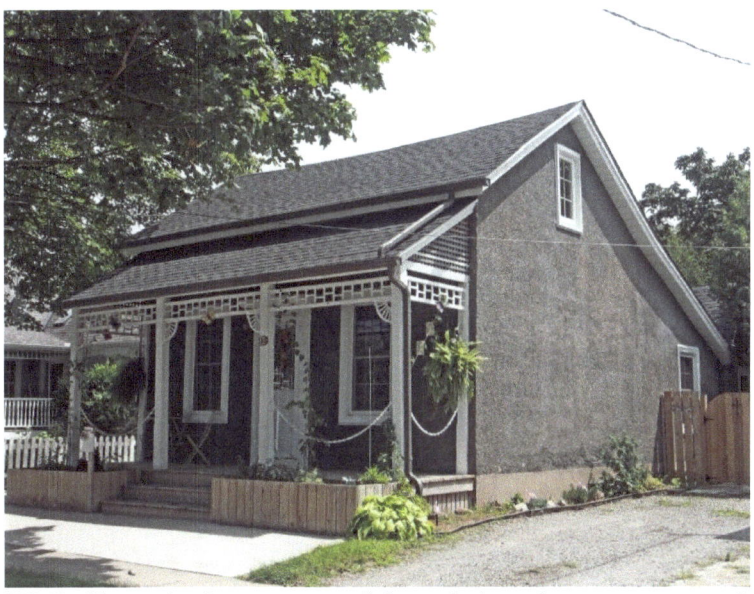

153 Dalhousie Avenue – saltbox, bric-a-brac on veranda

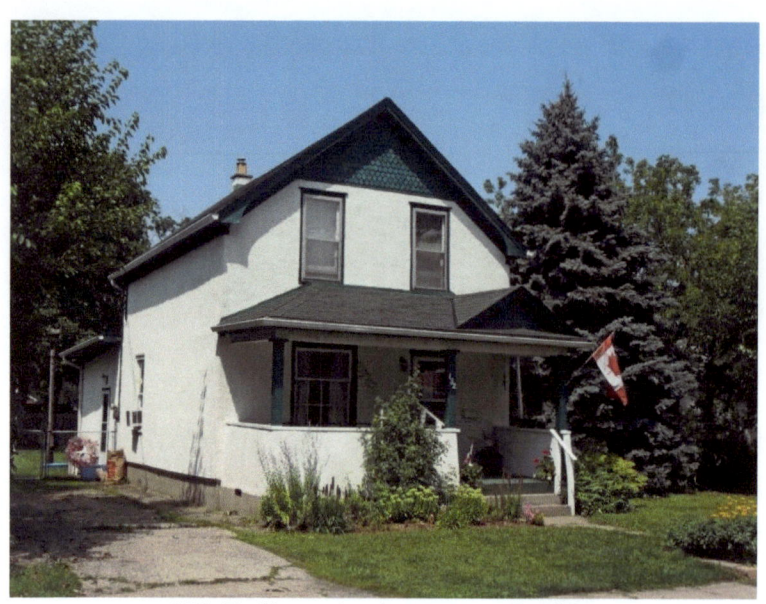

152 Dalhousie Avenue - Gothic

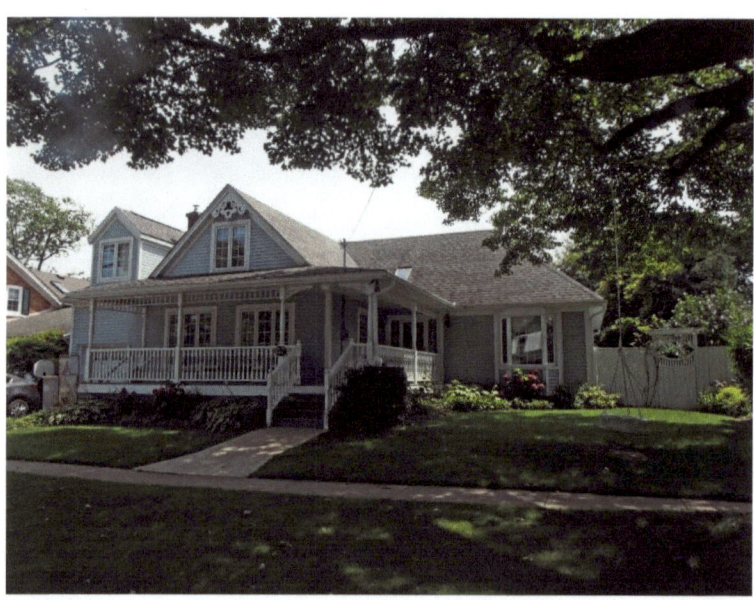

147 Dalhousie Avenue – Gothic, verge board trim on gable, dormer

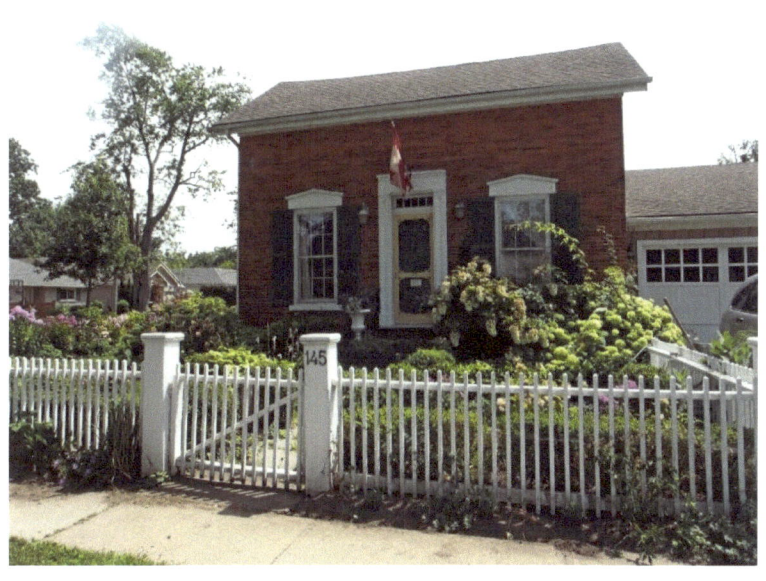

145 Dalhousie Avenue - Gothic

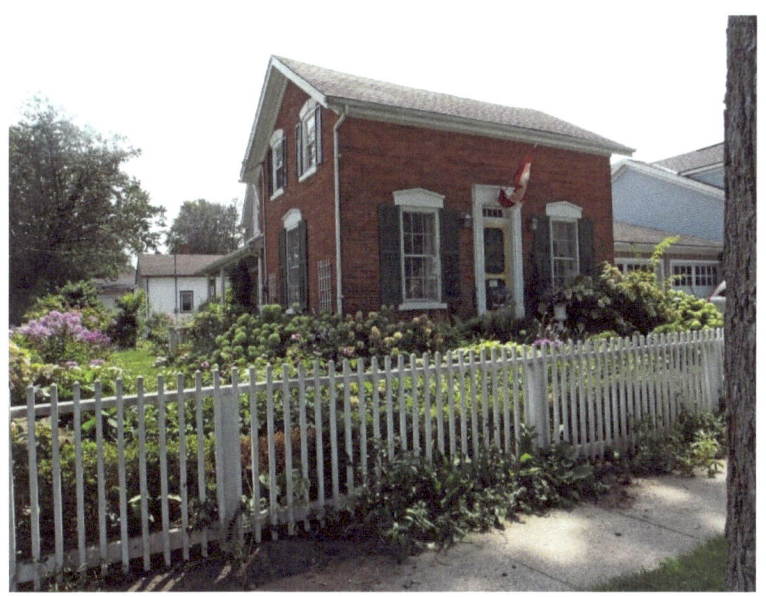

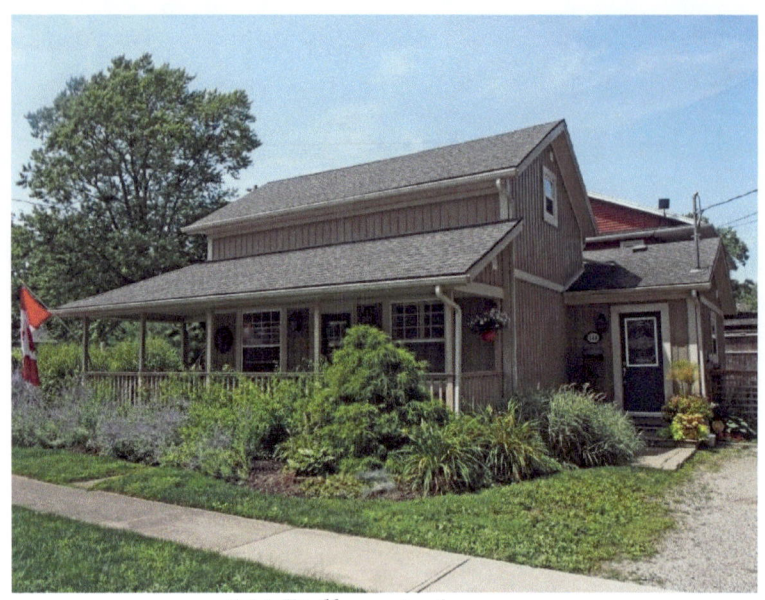

144 Dalhousie Avenue

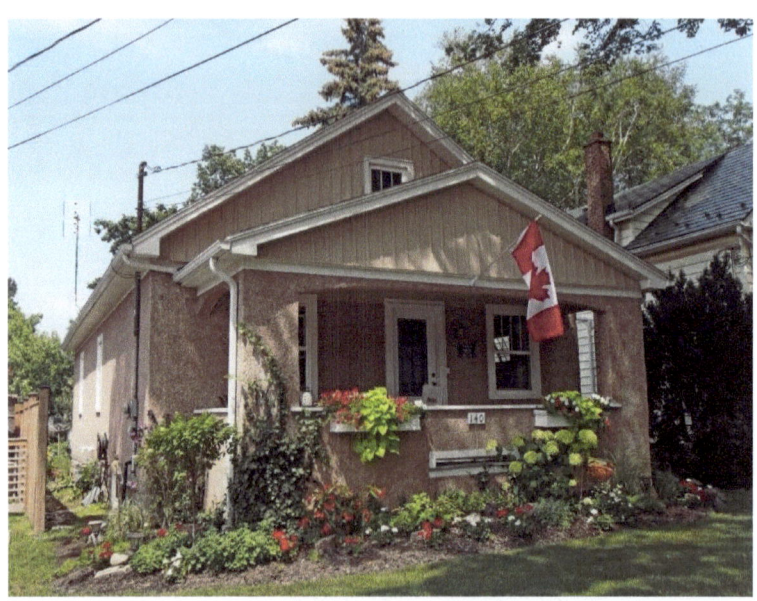

140 Dalhousie Avenue

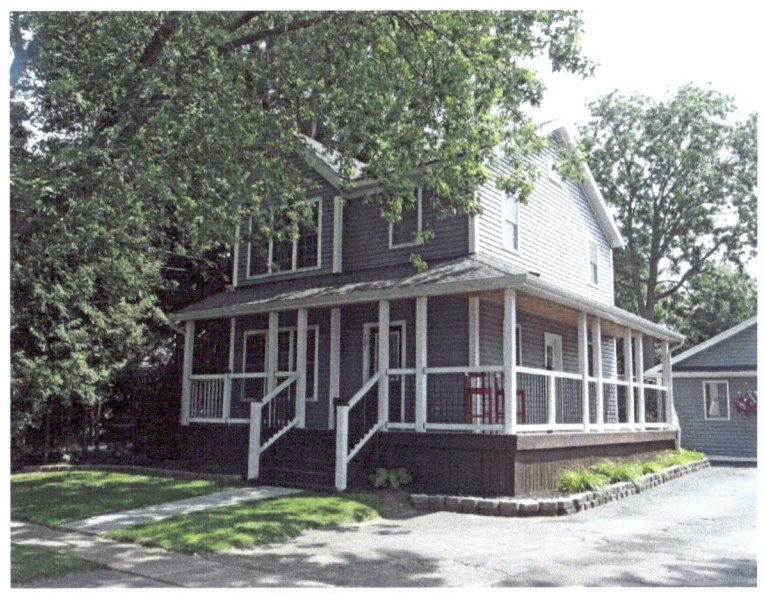
137 Dalhousie Avenue

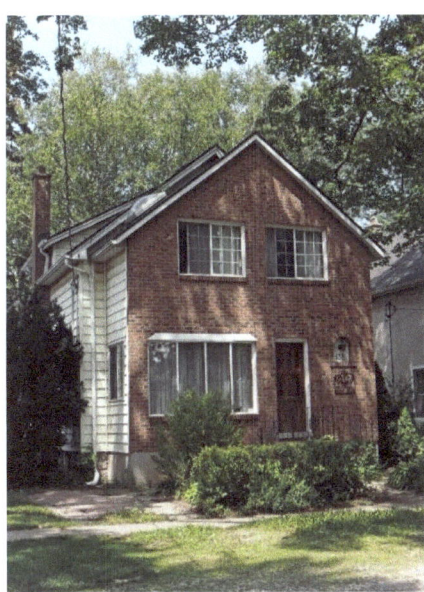
138 Dalhousie Avenue

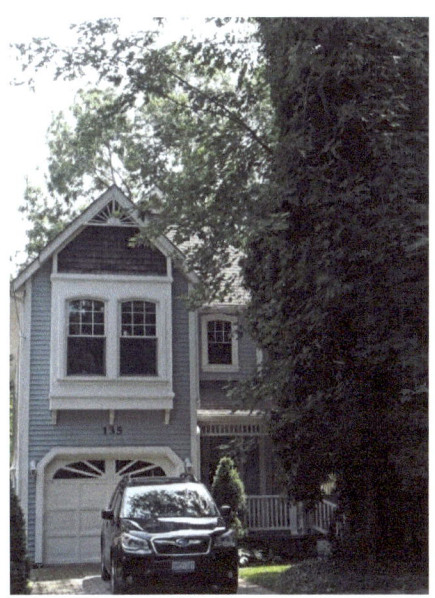
135 Dalhousie Avenue

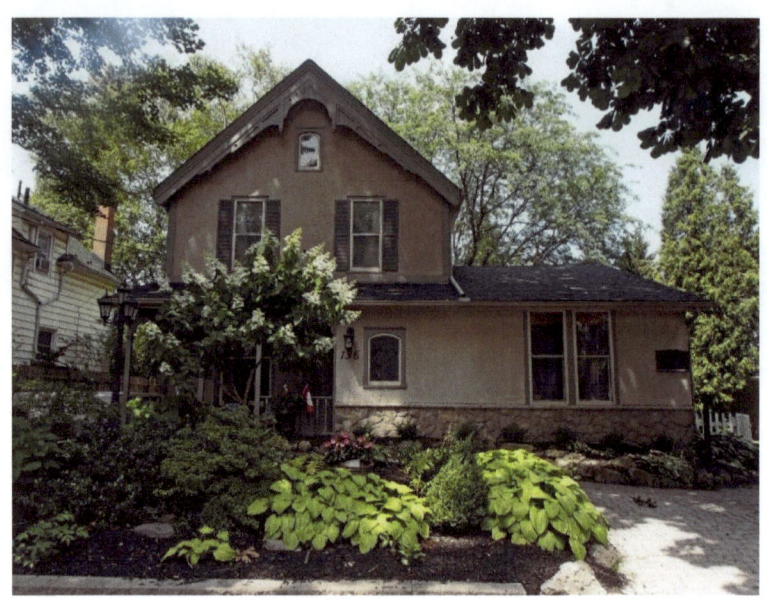

136 Dalhousie Avenue

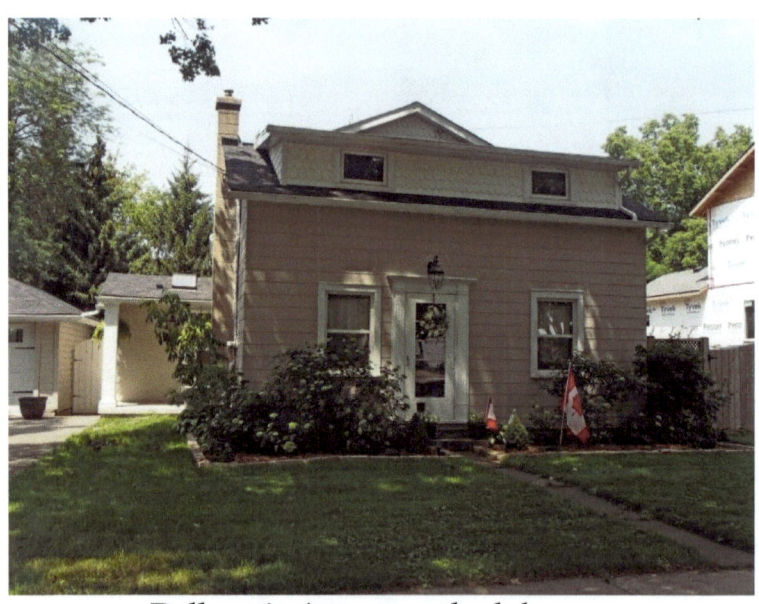

Dalhousie Avenue – shed dormer

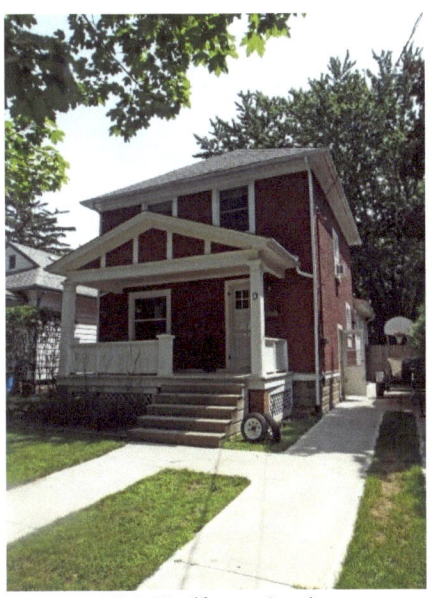

131 Dalhousie Avenue

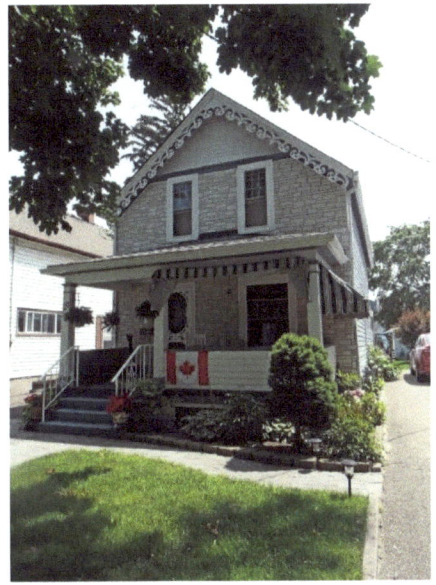

127 Dalhousie Avenue
Verge board trim on gable

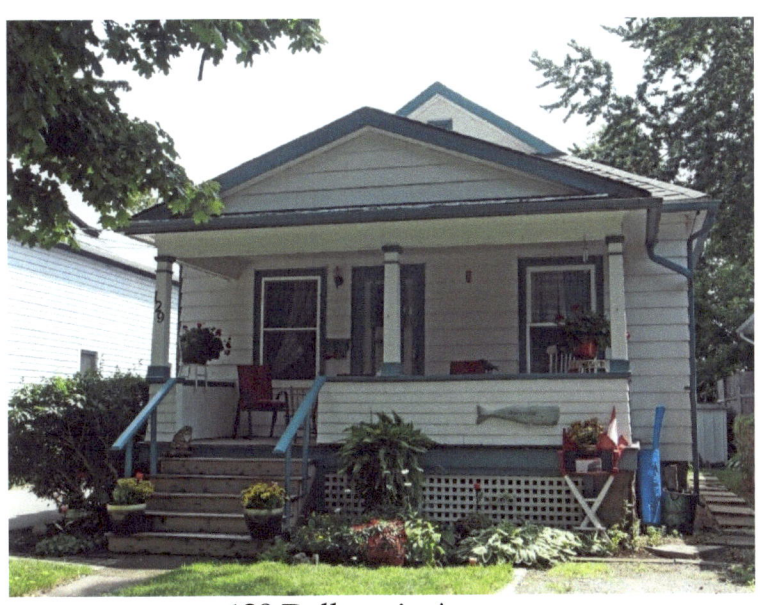

129 Dalhousie Avenue

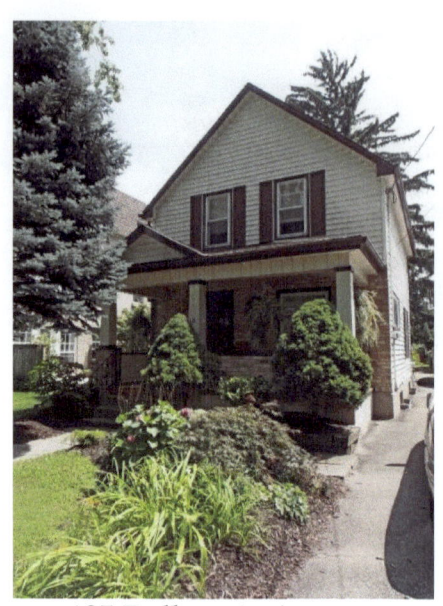

125 Dalhousie Avenue

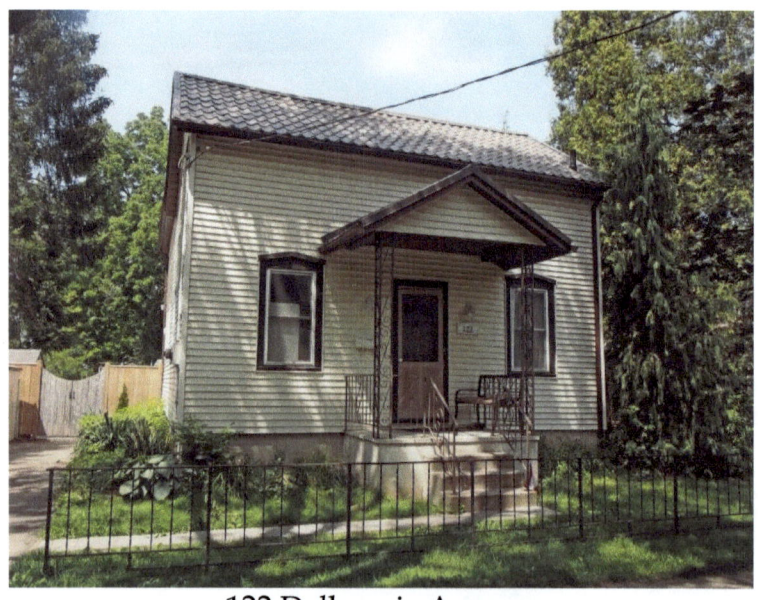

122 Dalhousie Avenue

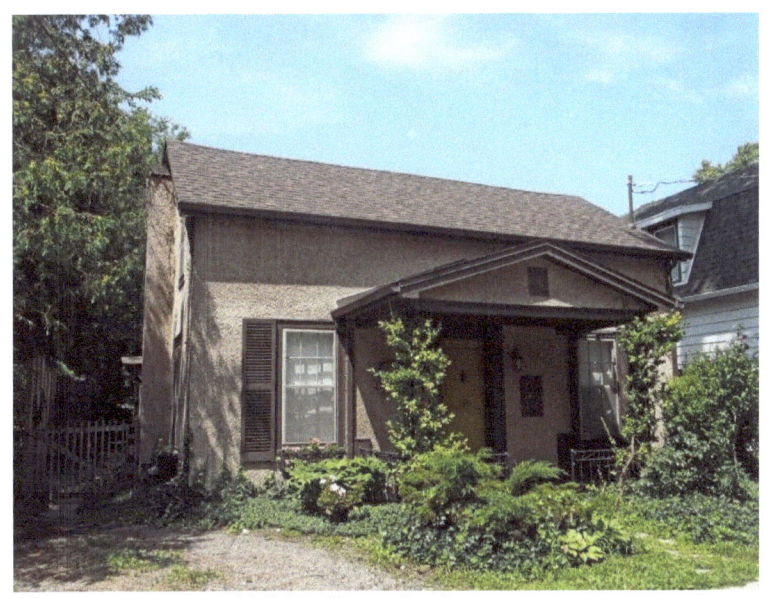

120 Dalhousie Avenue

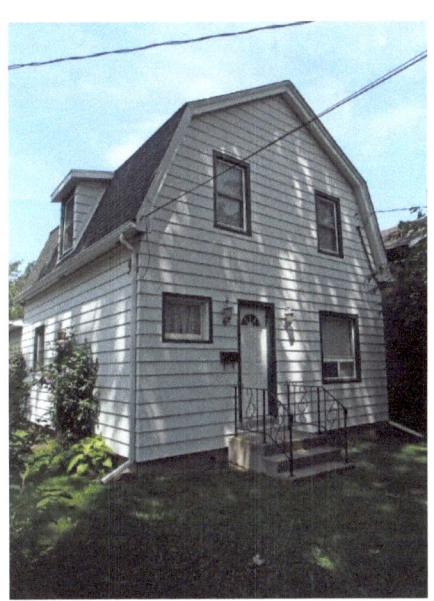

Dalhousie Avenue
Neo-Colonial, gambrel roof, dormer

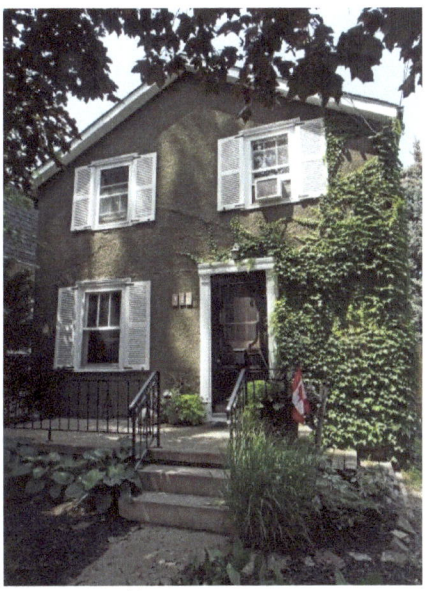

116 Dalhousie Avenue
Gothic

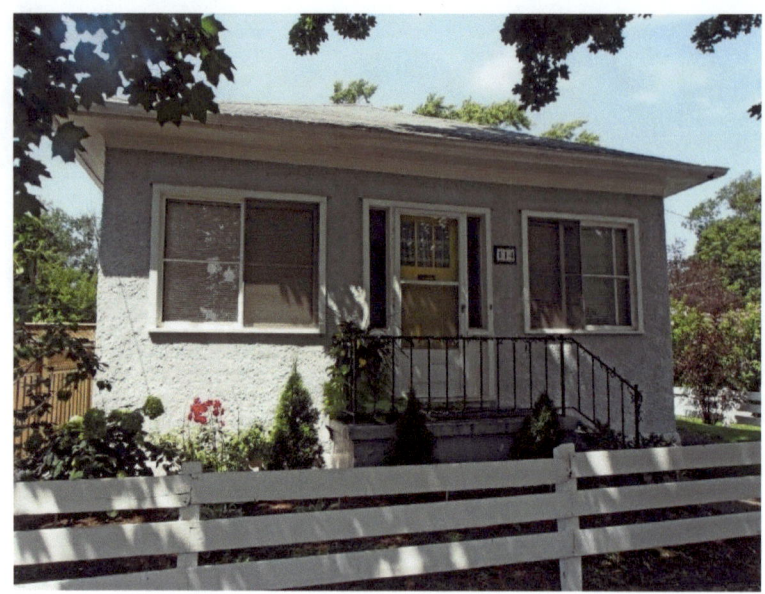
114 Dalhousie Avenue - Regency Cottage

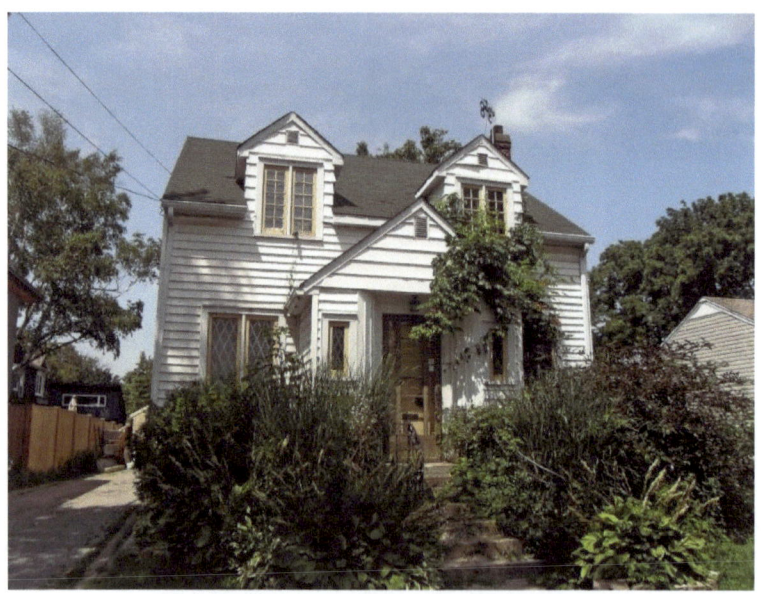
106 Dalhousie Avenue - dormers

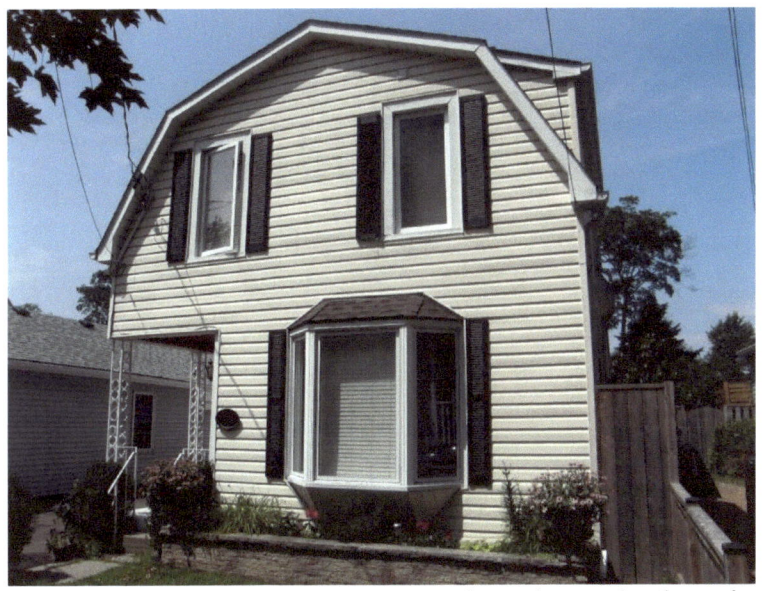

94 Dalhousie Avenue – Neo-Colonial, gambrel roof

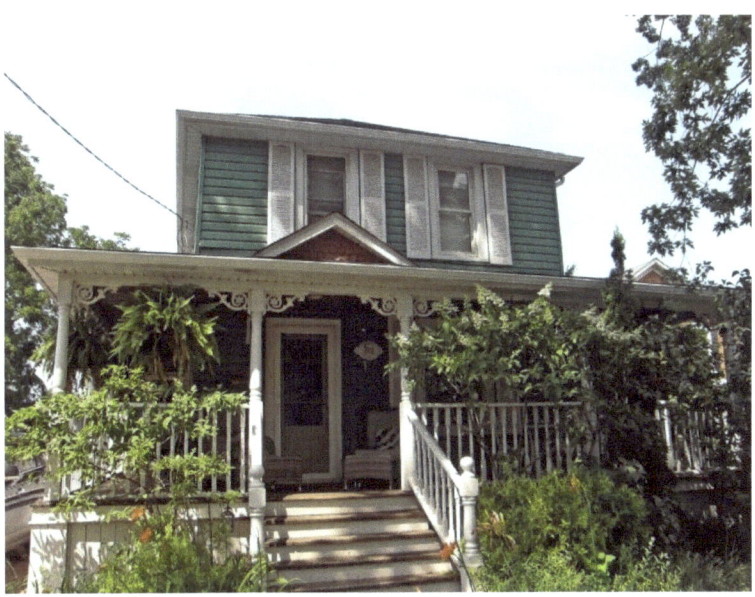

92 Dalhousie Avenue – two-storey home, bric-a-brac on wraparound veranda

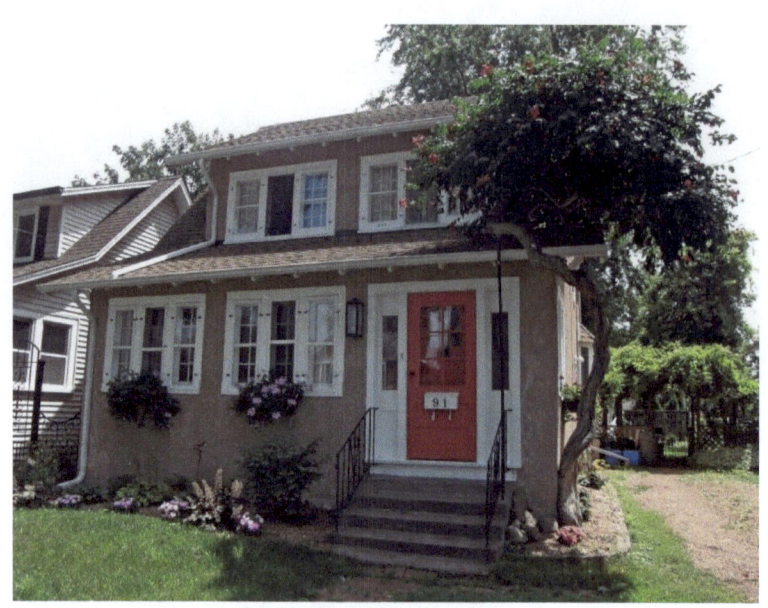

91 Dalhousie Avenue

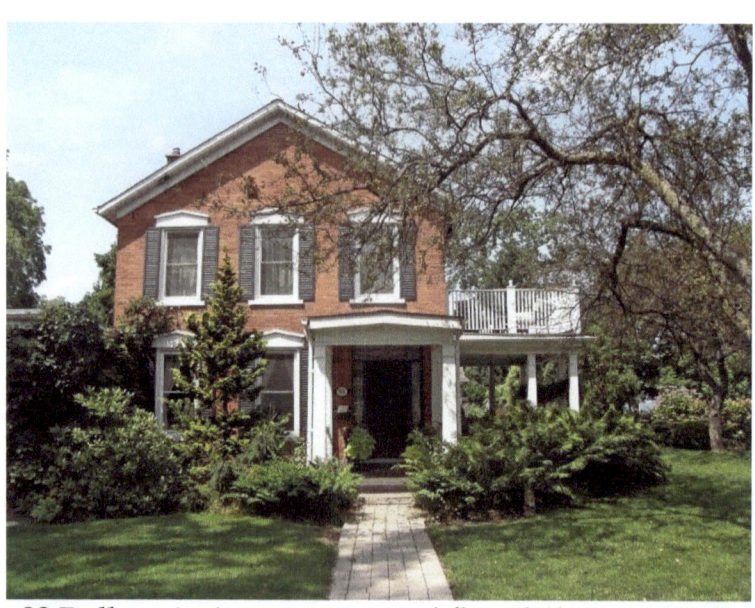

88 Dalhousie Avenue – second floor balcony on side

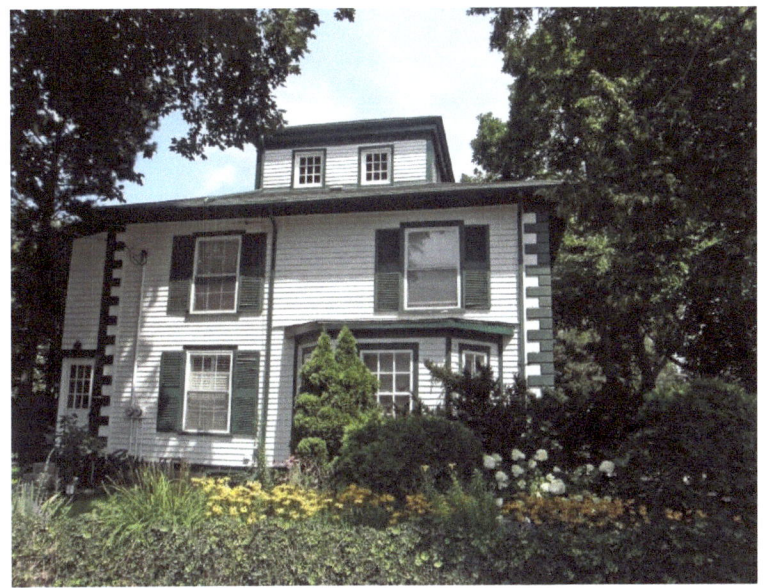

82 Dalhousie Avenue – dormer, corner quoins, bay window

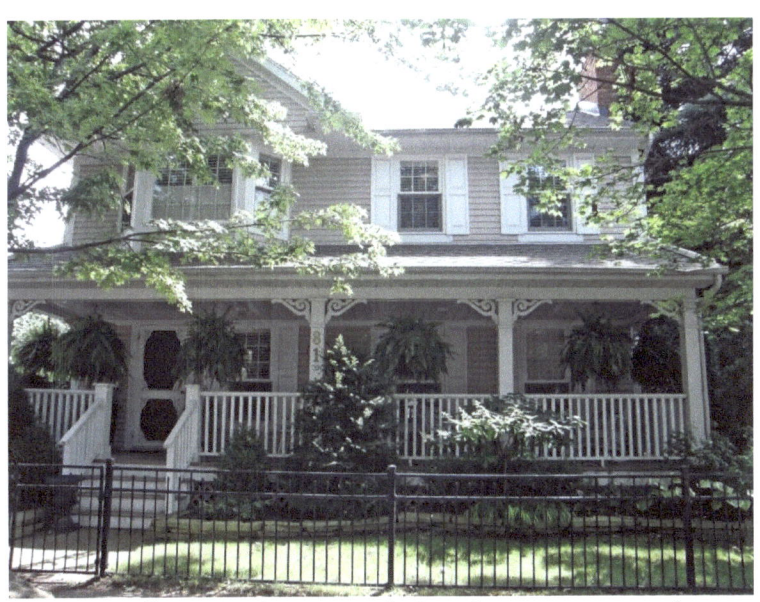

81 Dalhousie Avenue - bric-a-brac on veranda

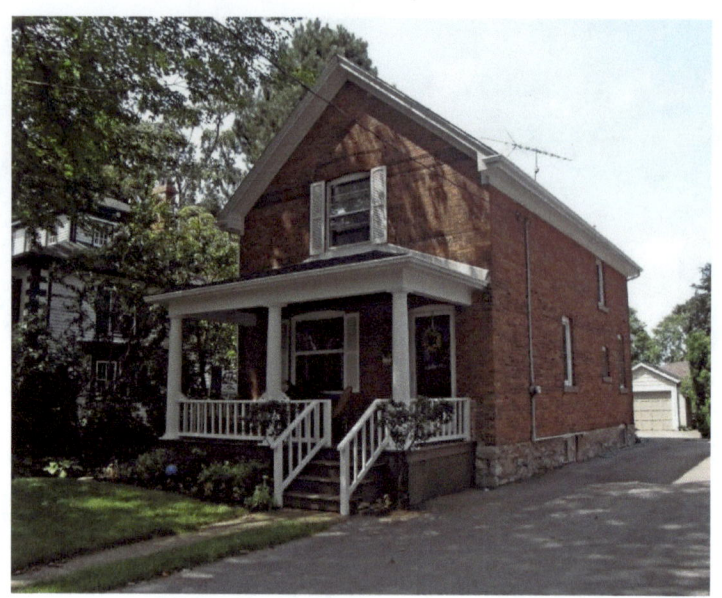

80 Dalhousie Avenue - Gothic

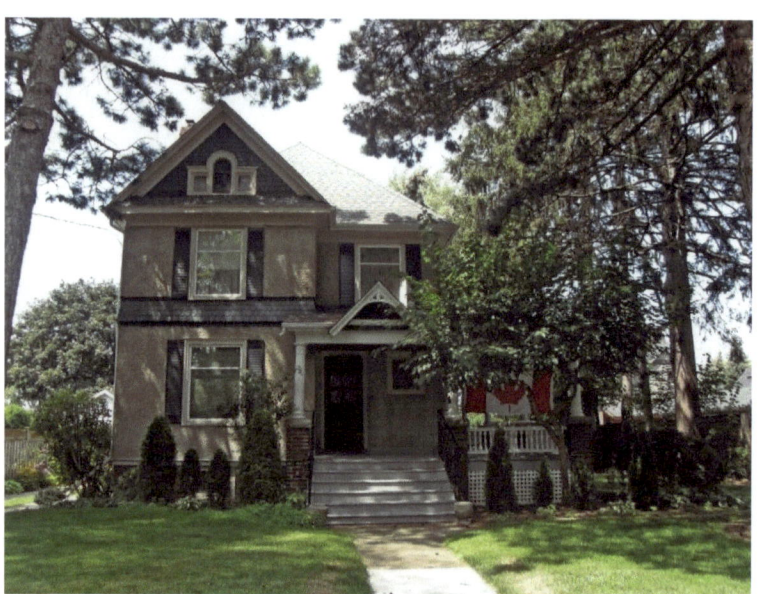

76 Dalhousie Avenue – Palladian window in gable

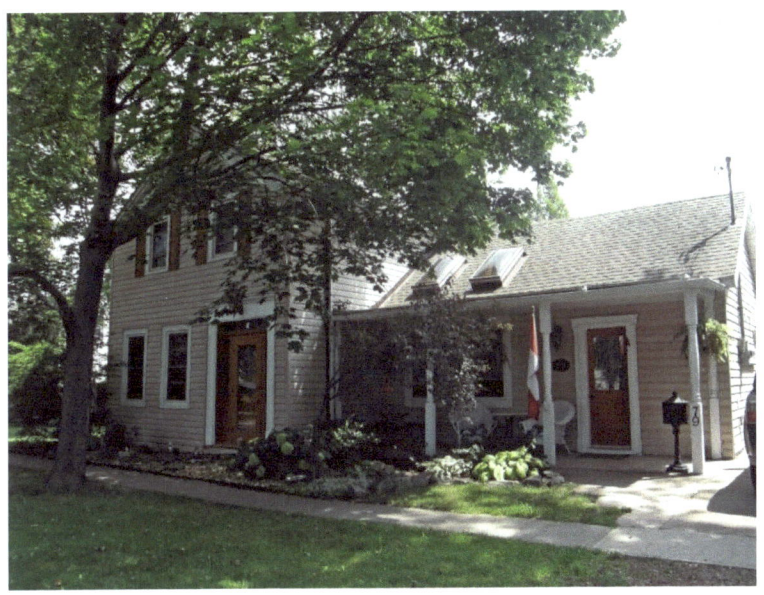

79 Dalhousie Avenue

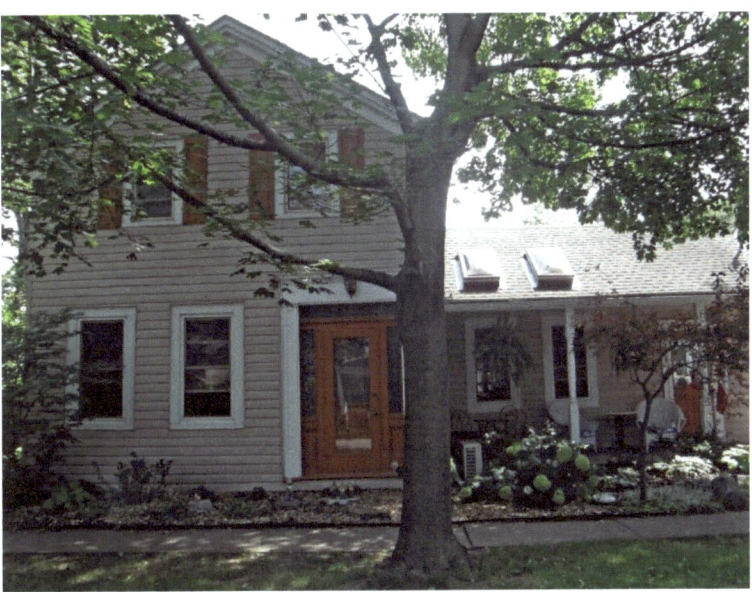

Dalhousie Avenue – two storeys with a one storey wing

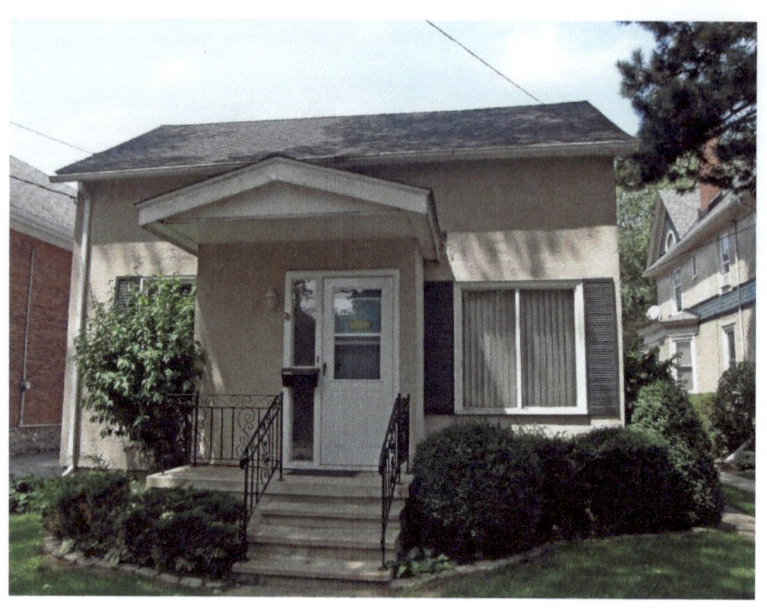

78 Dalhousie Avenue – Regency cottage

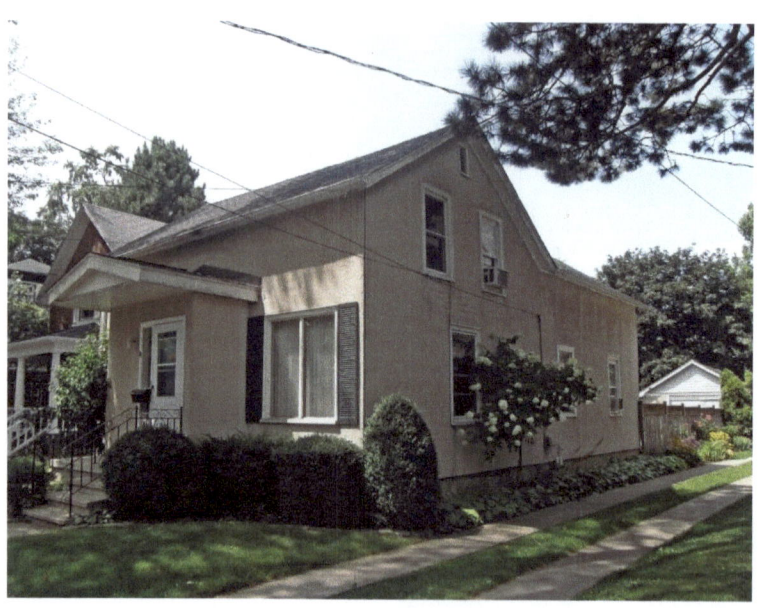

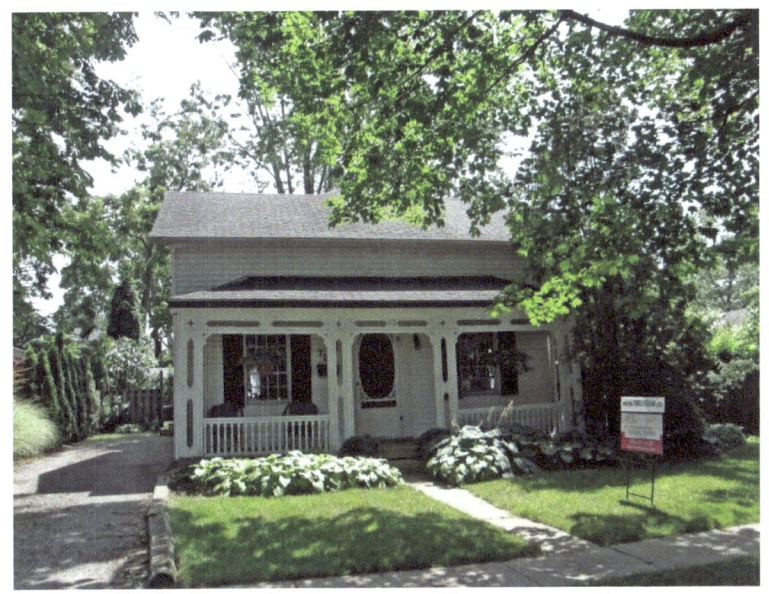

75 Dalhousie Avenue – Regency cottage

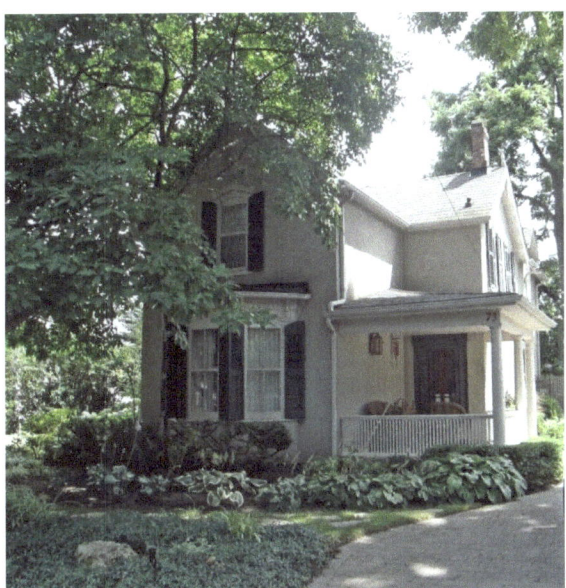

73 Dalhousie Avenue - Gothic

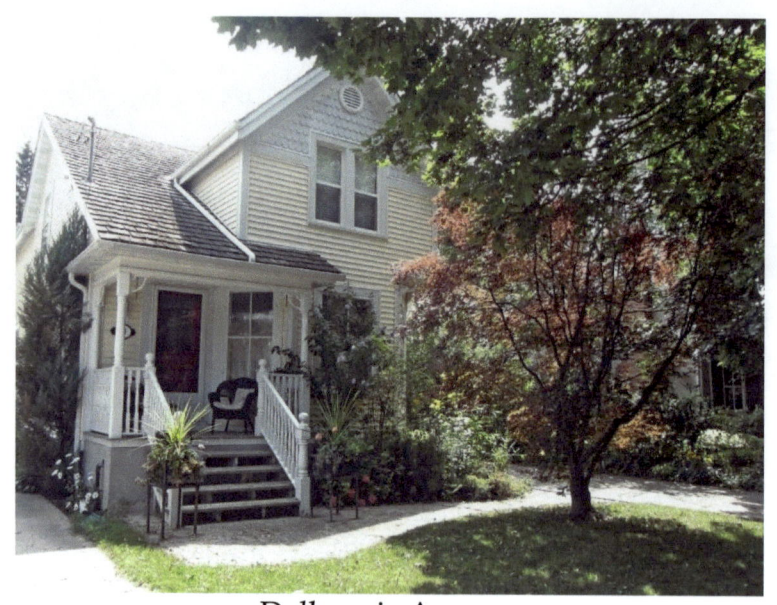

Dalhousie Avenue

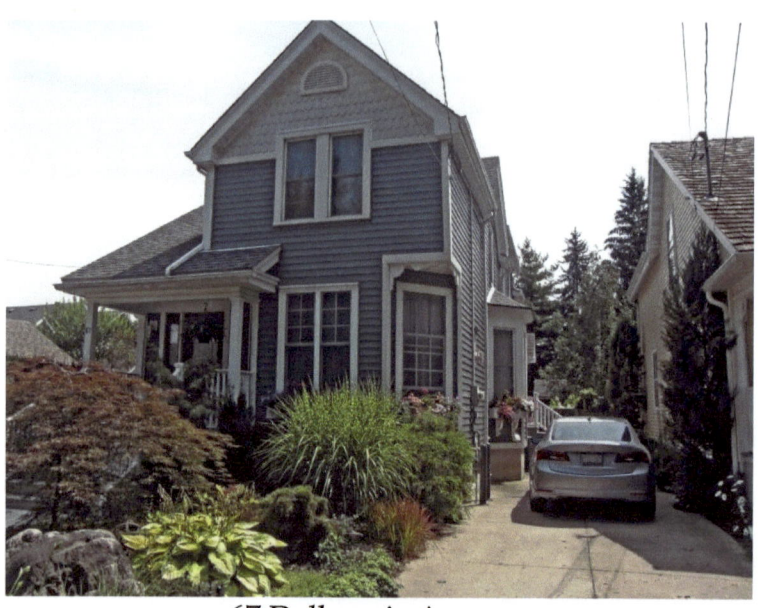

67 Dalhousie Avenue

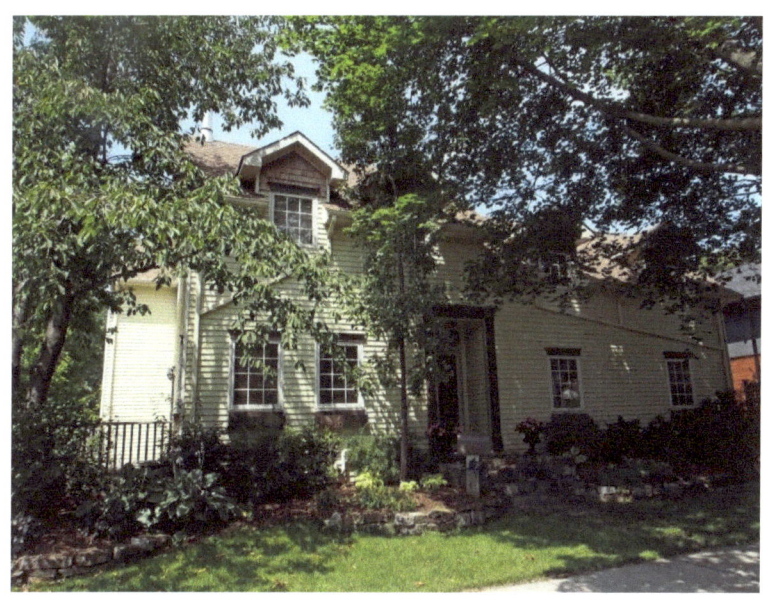

Dalhousie Avenue - dormers

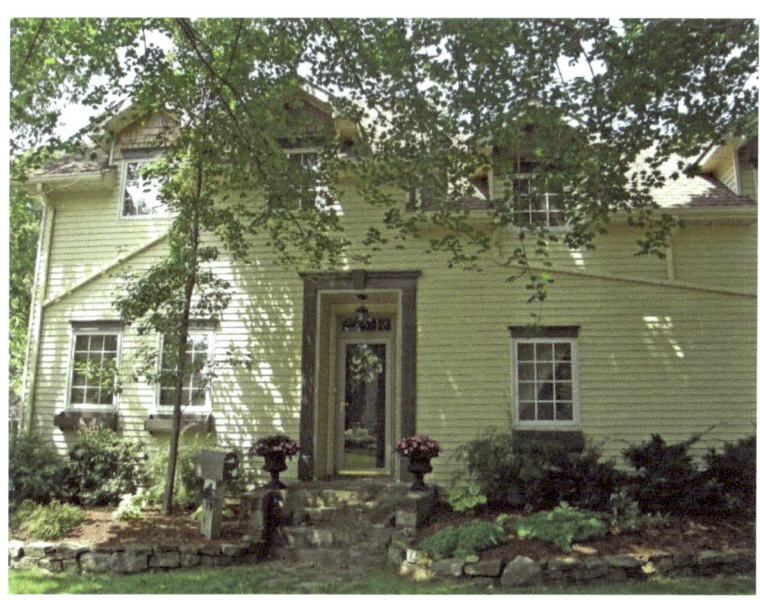

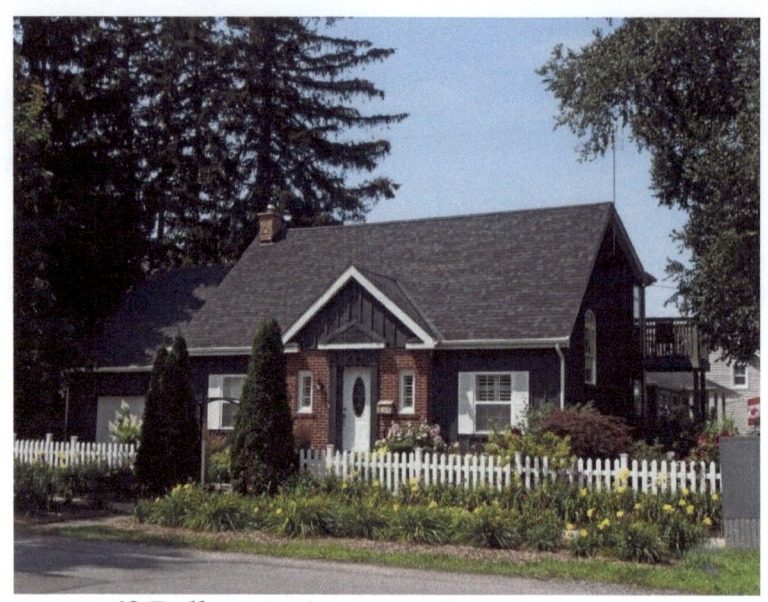
62 Dalhousie Avenue – Regency cottage

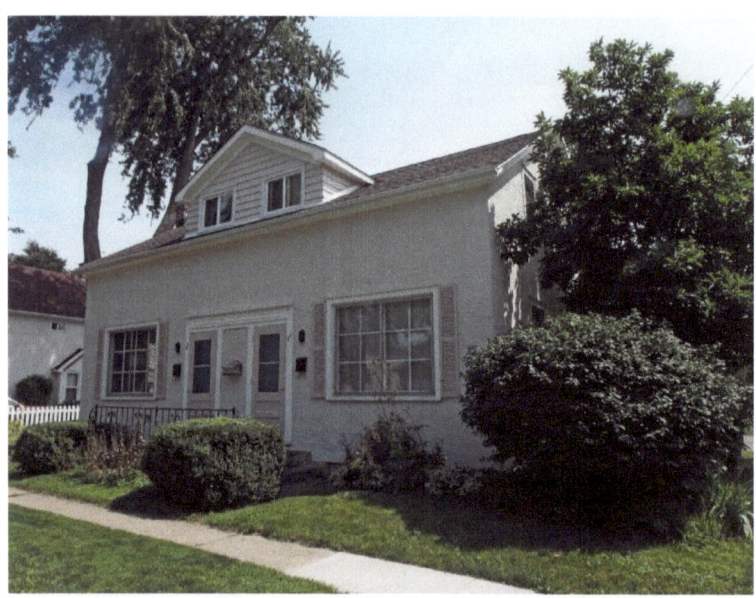
59 Dalhousie Avenue – Regency cottage with dormer

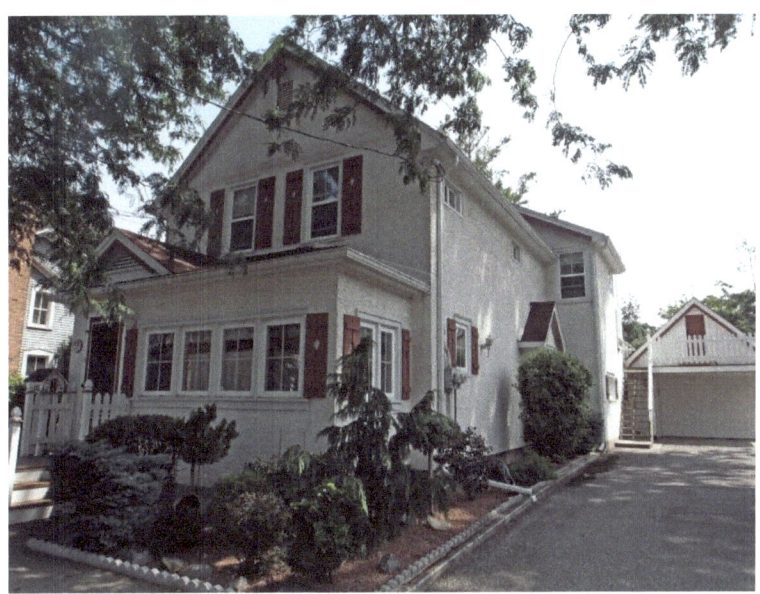

55 Dalhousie Avenue - Gothic

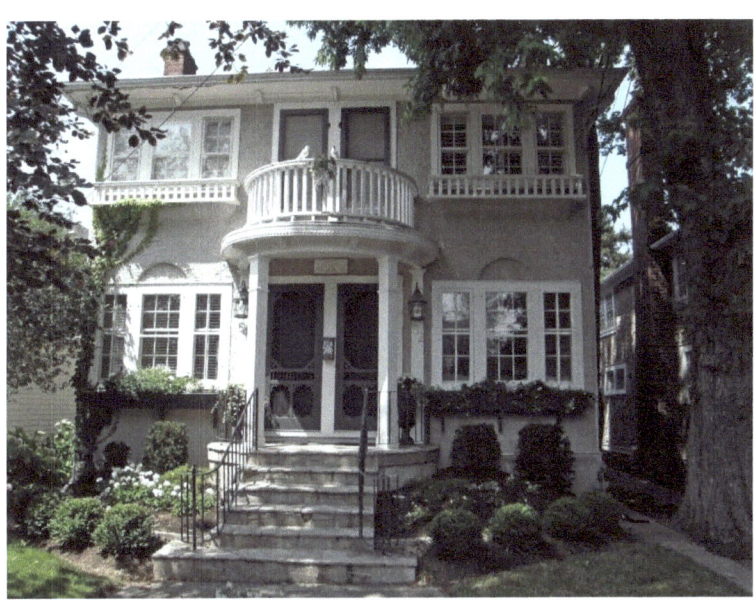

52 Dalhousie Avenue – Neo-Classical – two storeys, symmetrical façade, second floor semi-circular balcony above pillared porch

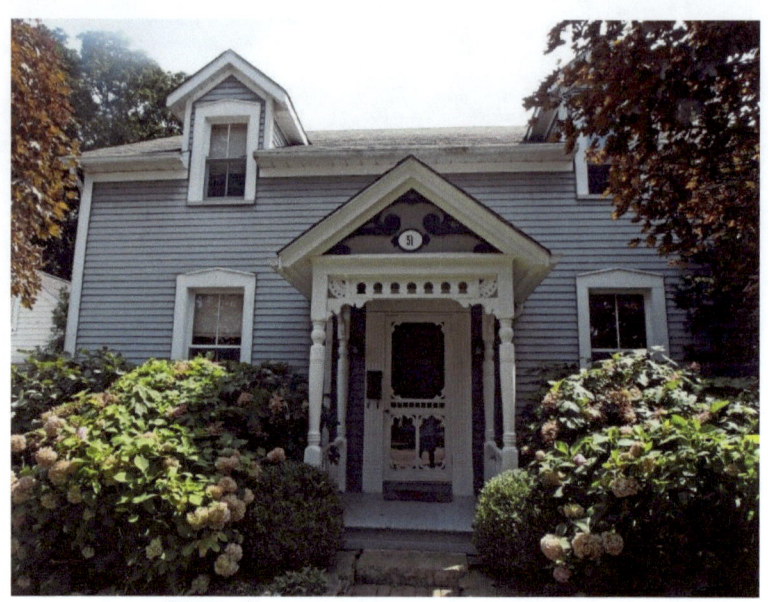

51 Dalhousie Avenue - dormers

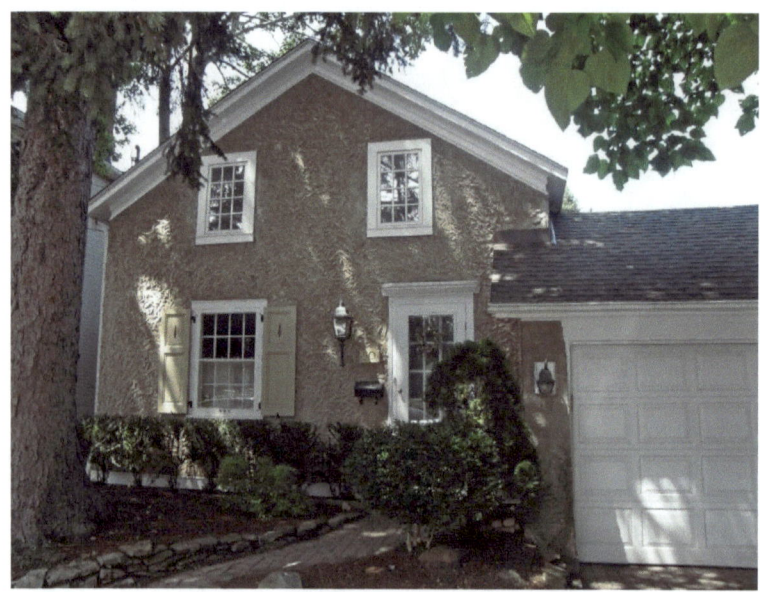

50 Dalhousie Avenue - Gothic

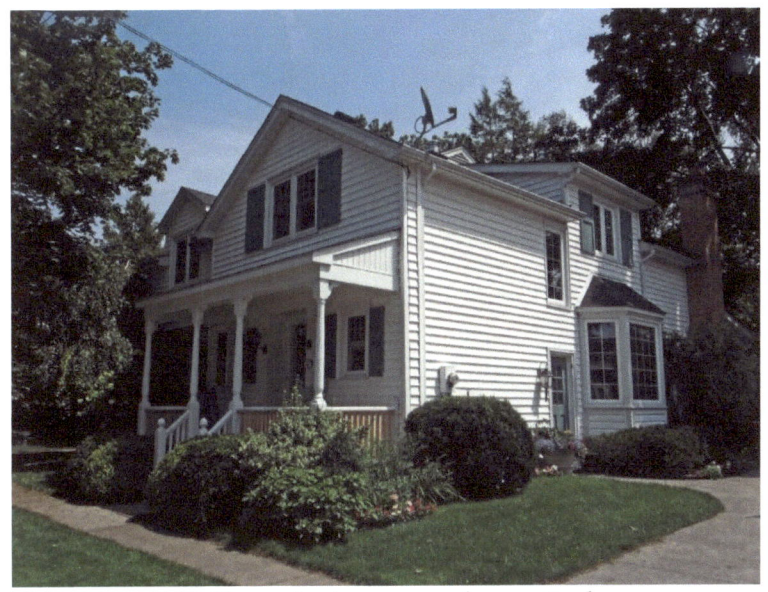

47 Dalhousie Avenue – bay window

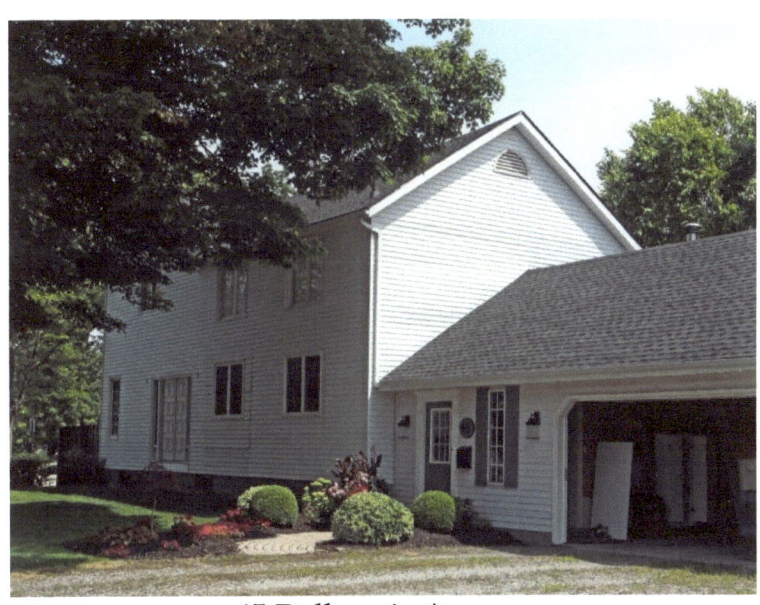

45 Dalhousie Avenue

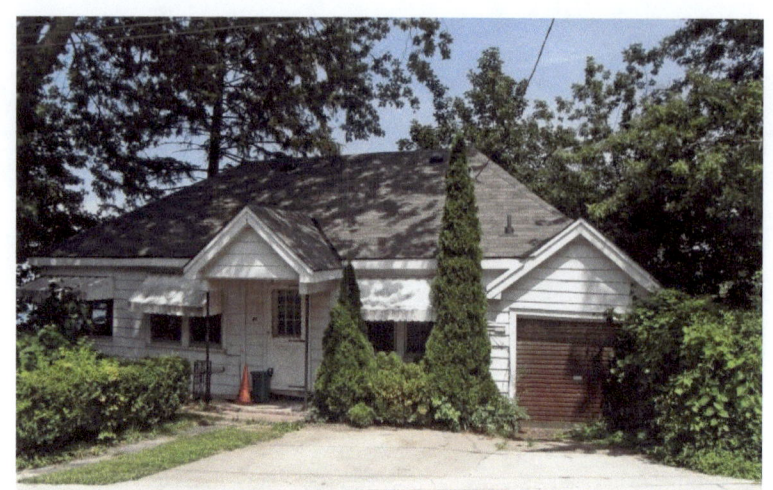

44 Dalhousie Avenue – Regency cottage

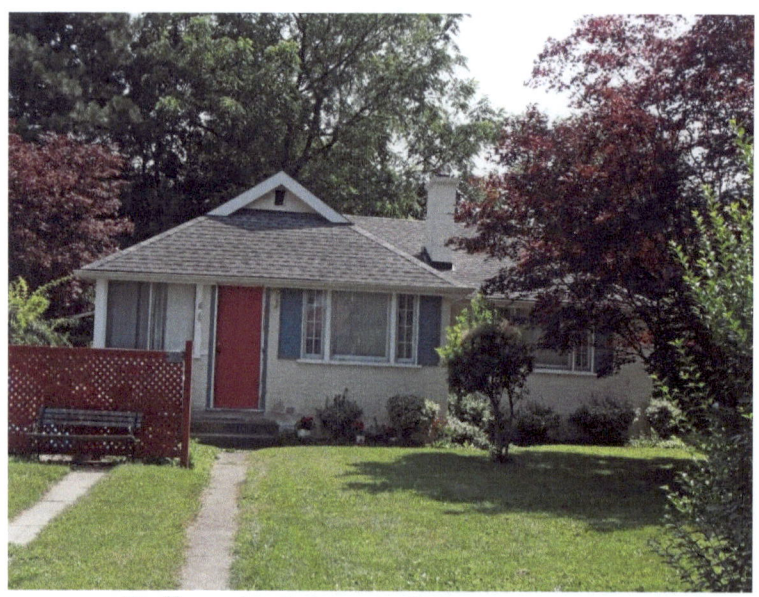

Dalhousie Avenue – Regency cottage

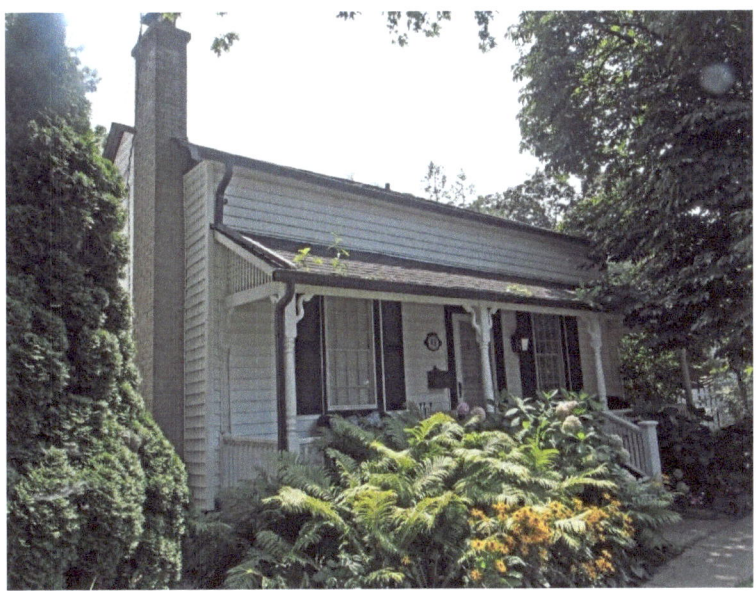
43 Dalhousie Avenue – Alexander Muir House c. 1840

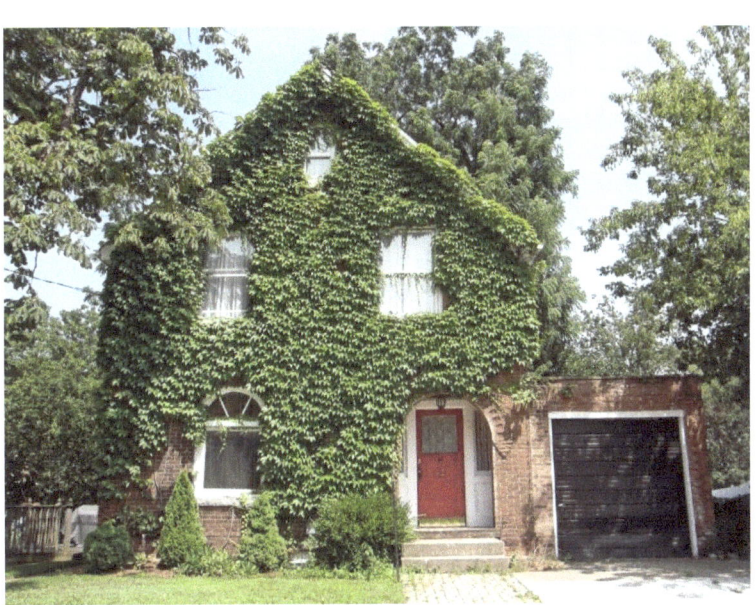
42 Dalhousie Avenue - Gothic

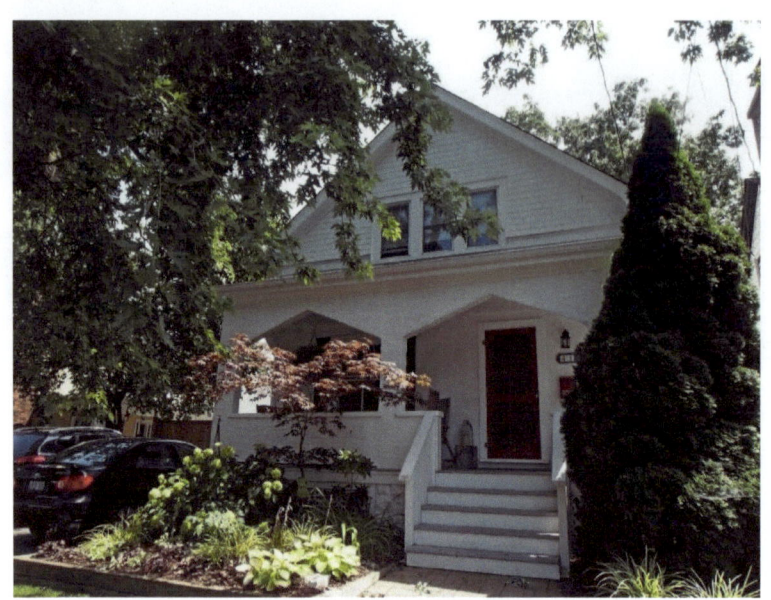

41 Dalhousie Avenue

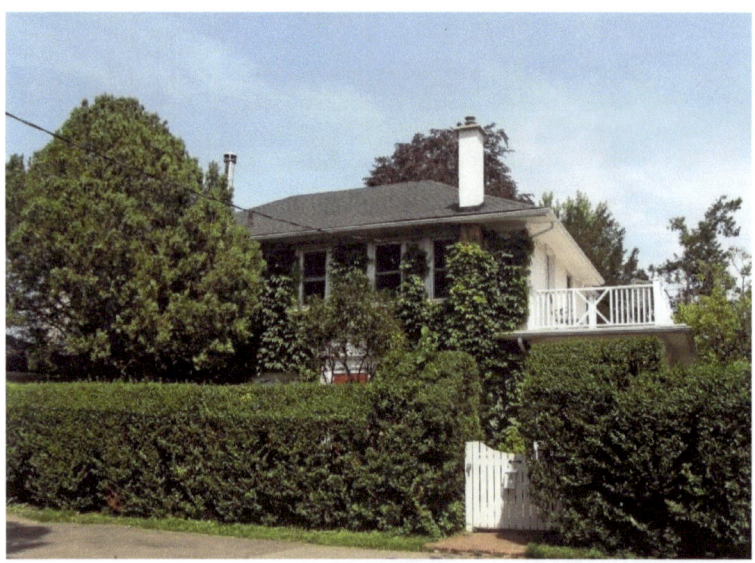

36 Dalhousie Avenue – hipped roof, second floor balcony

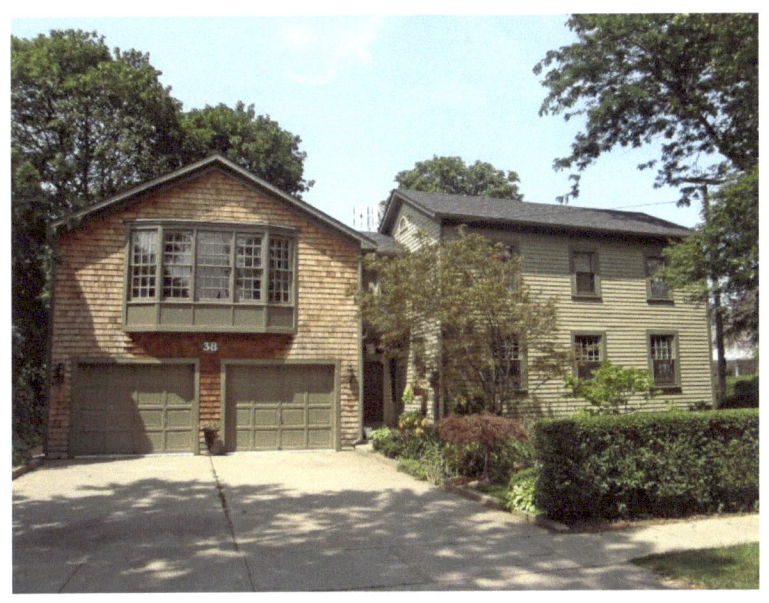

38 Dalhousie Avenue

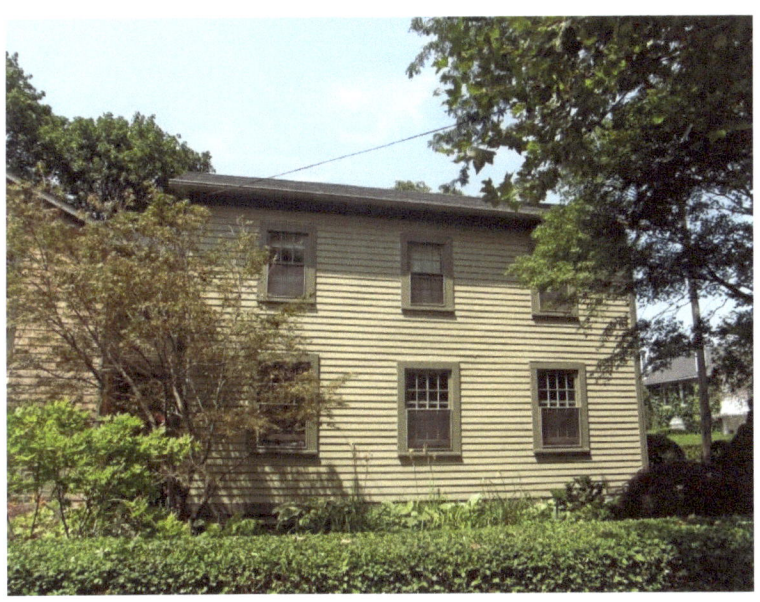

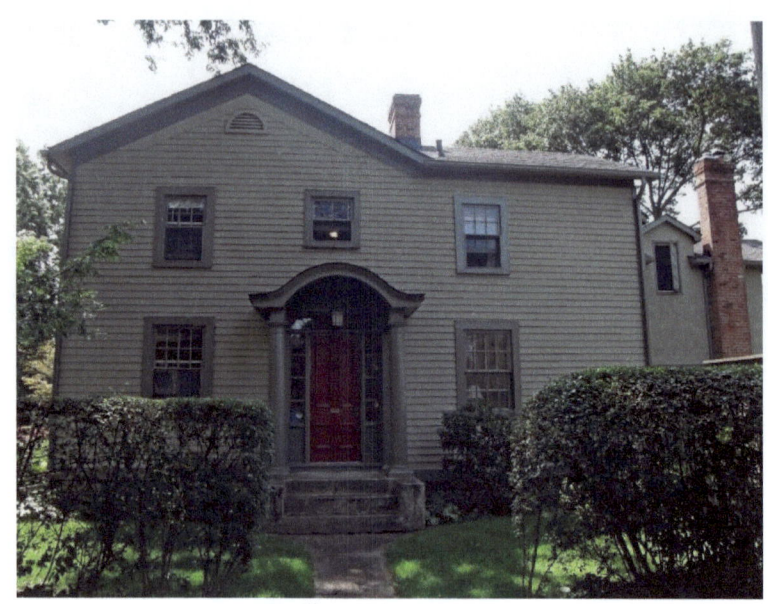

Dalhousie Avenue

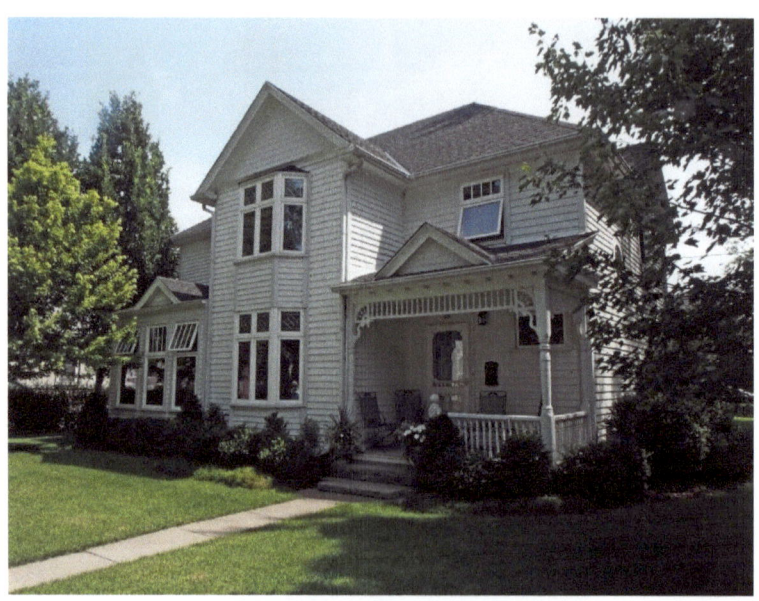

33 Dalhousie Avenue

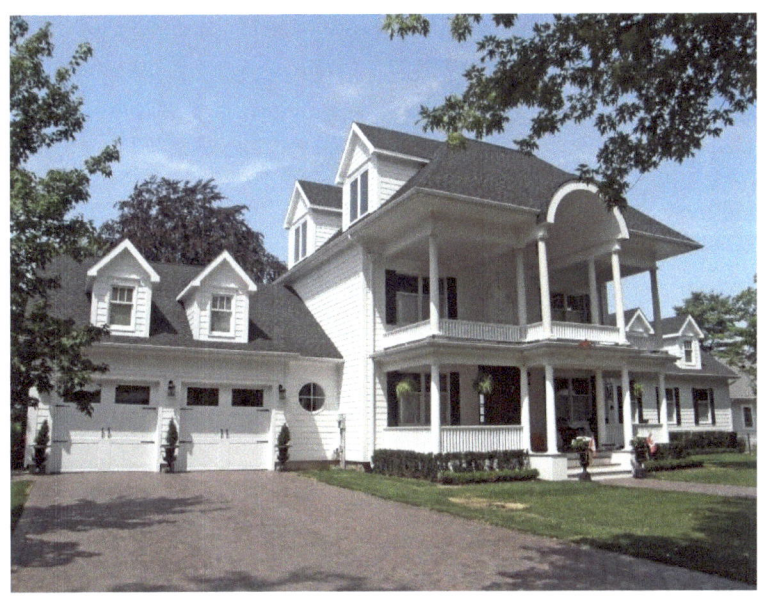

Dalhousie Avenue – sidelights and transom windows, two-storey verandah with Doric pillars and open balustrade, dormers in roof

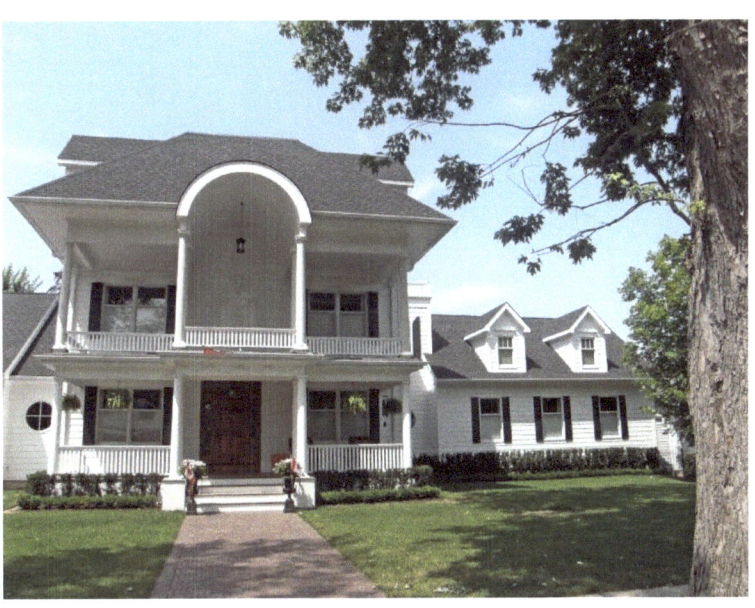

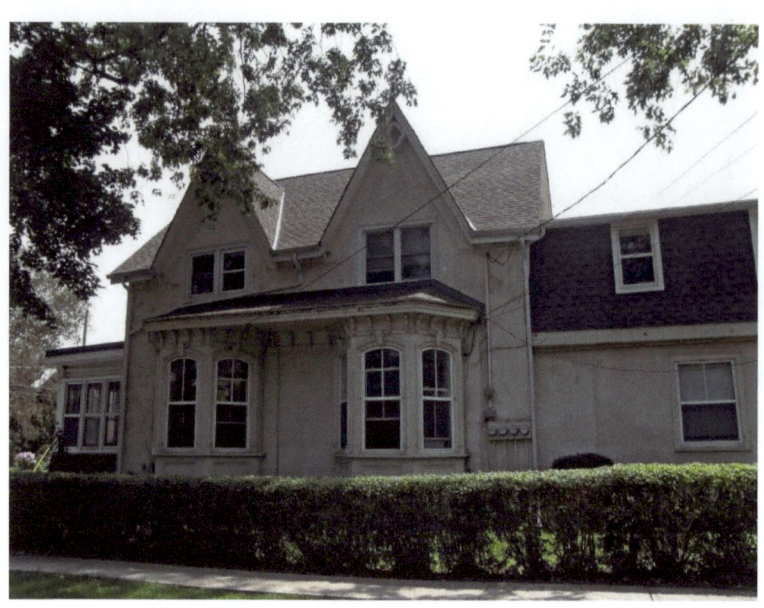

29 Dalhousie Avenue – Gothic Revival, verge board trim on gables, cornice brackets above bay windows

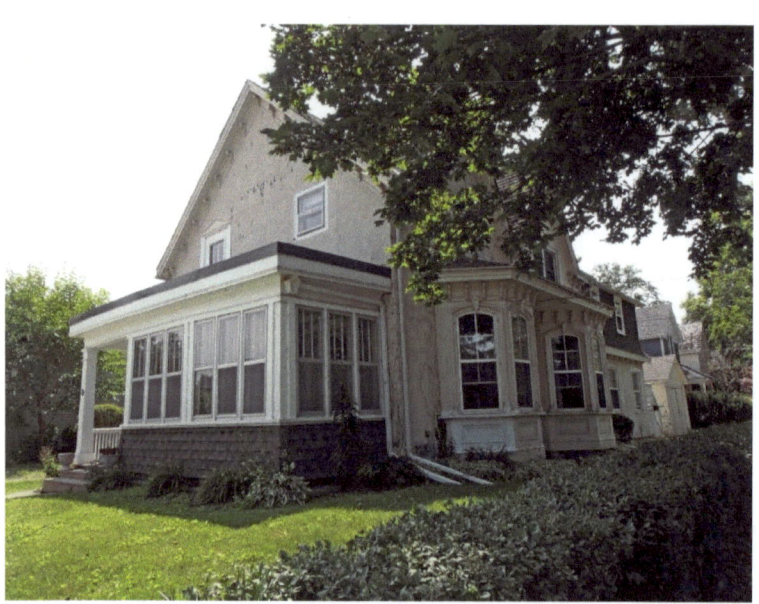

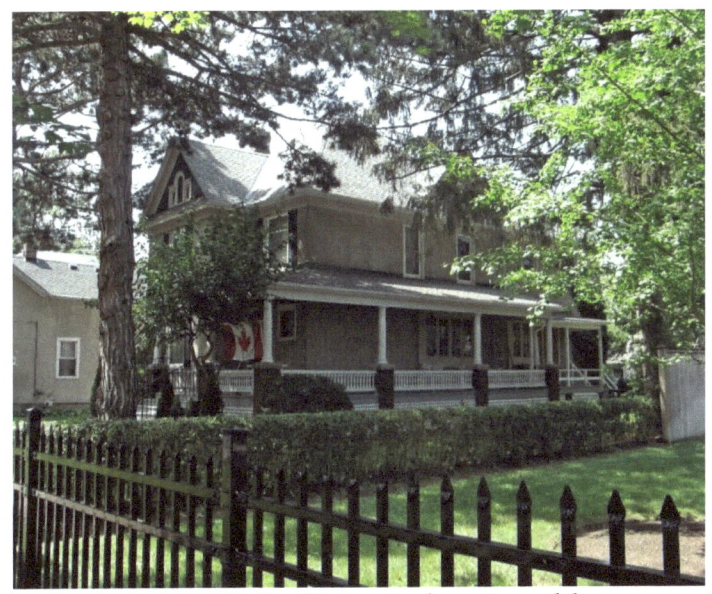

Dalhousie Avenue – Palladian window in gable, wraparound veranda with Doric pillars and open balustrade

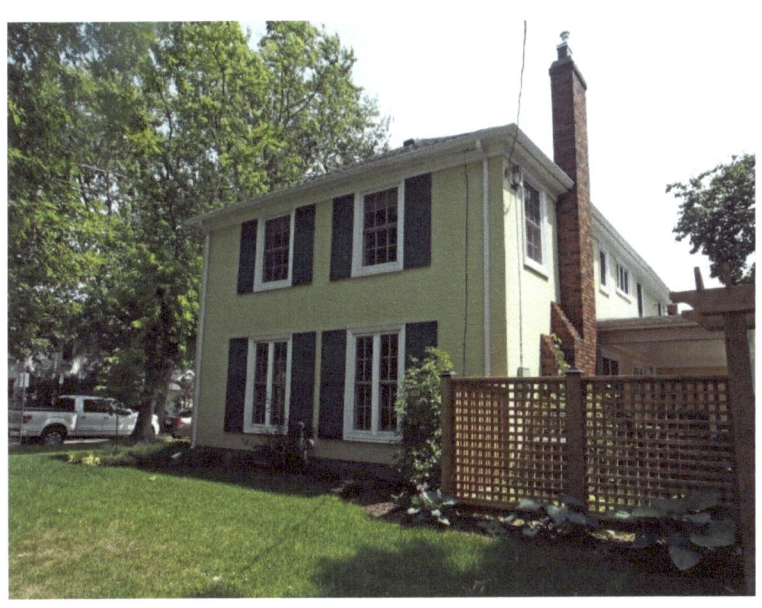

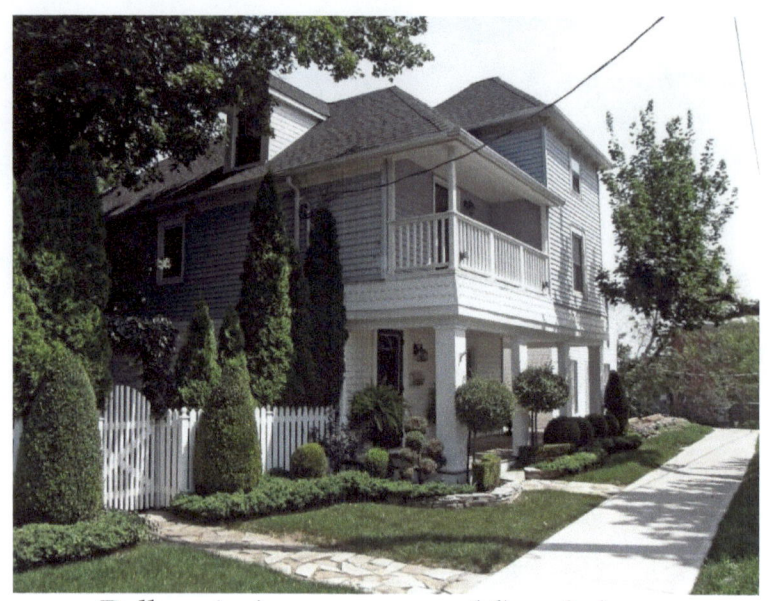
Dalhousie Avenue – second floor balcony

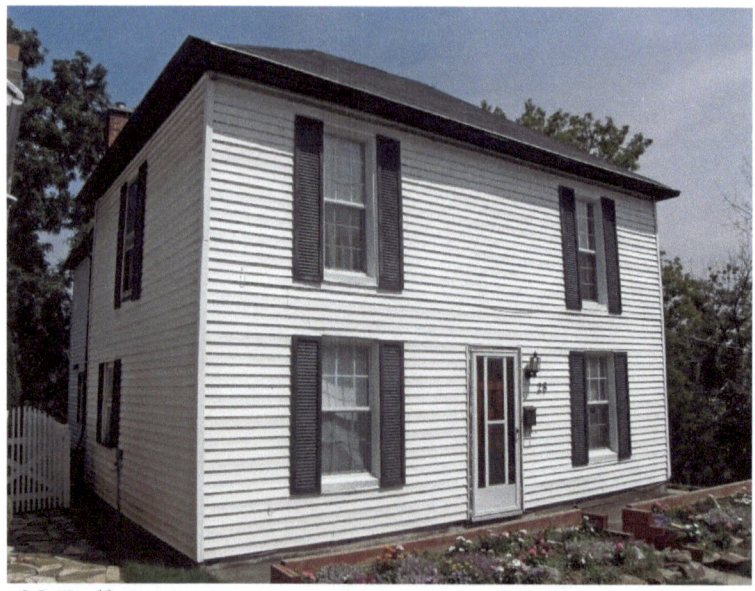
28 Dalhousie Avenue – hipped roof, balanced façade

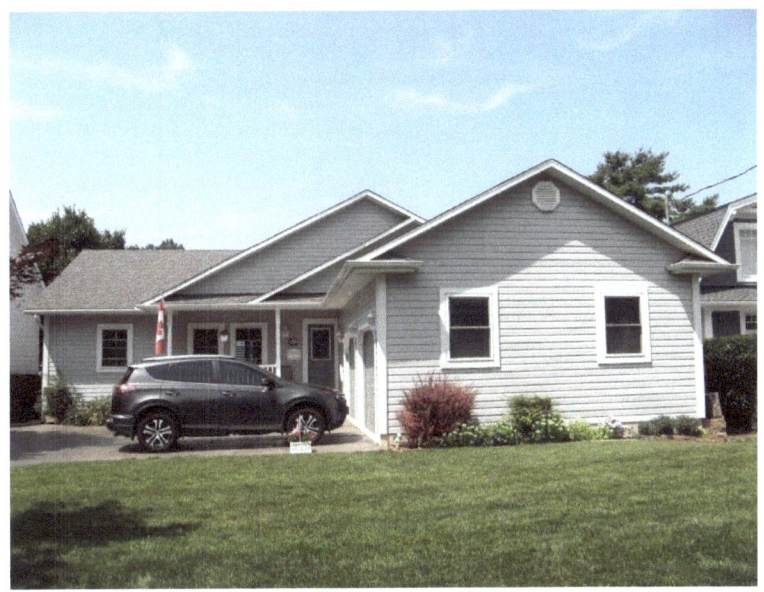

26 Dalhousie Avenue

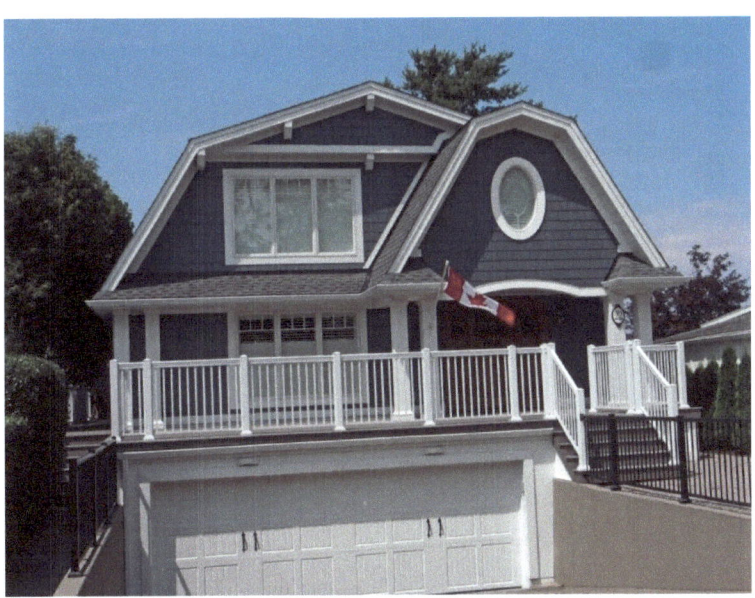

22 Dalhousie Avenue – Neo-Colonial – gambrel roof

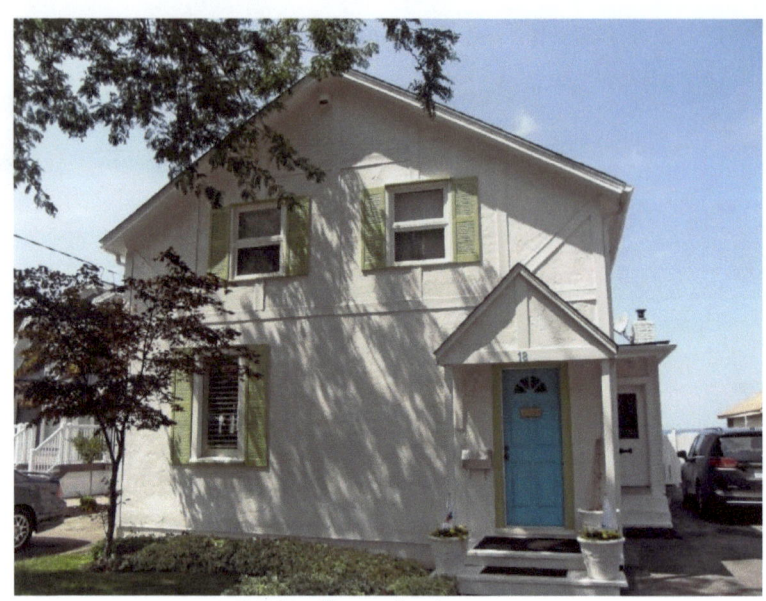

18 Dalhousie Avenue

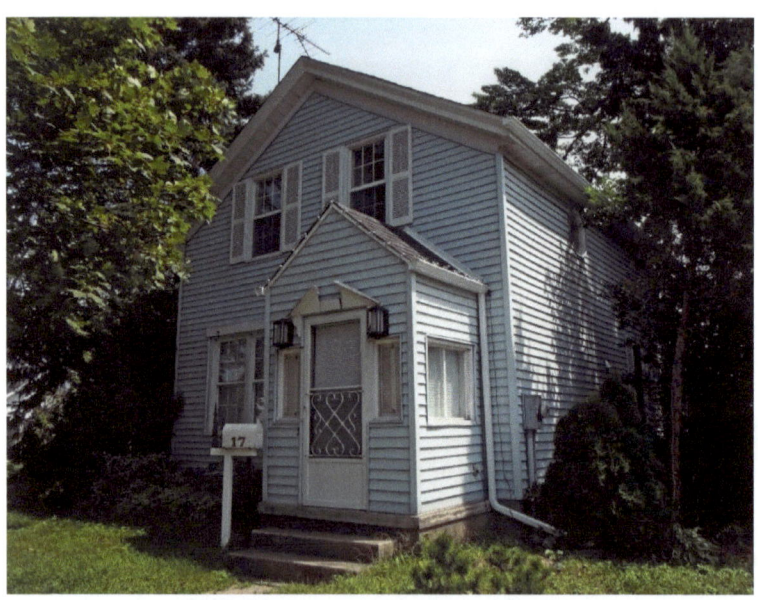

17 Dalhousie Avenue - Gothic

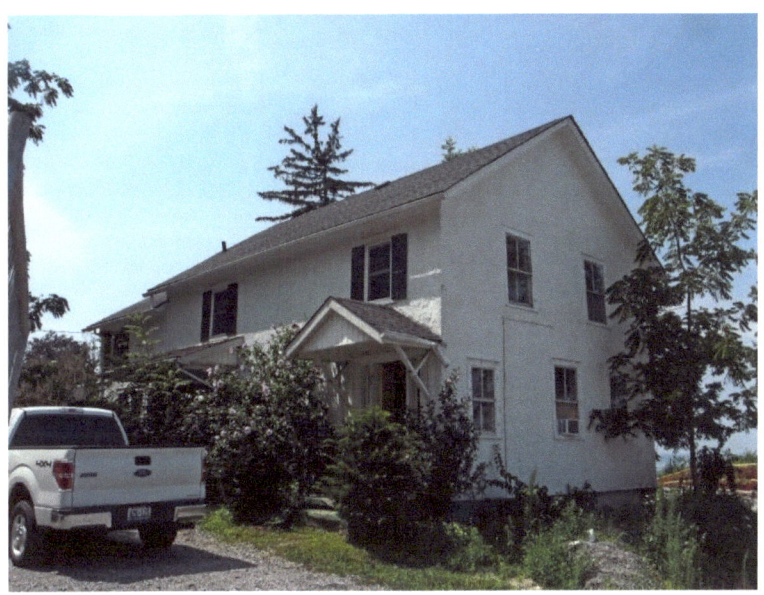

Dalhousie Avenue

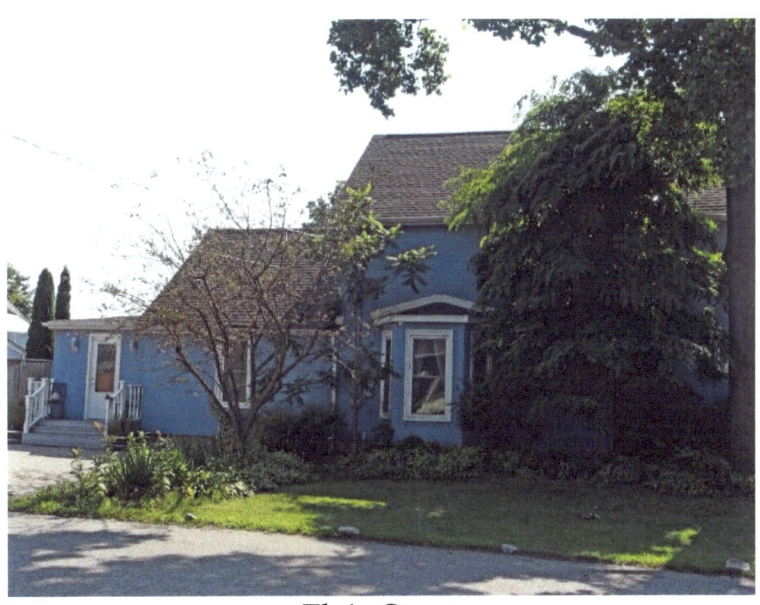

Elgin Street

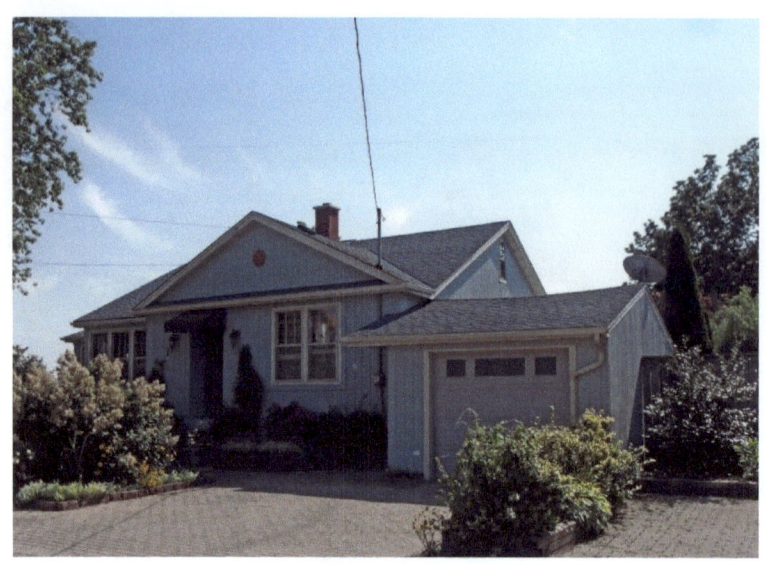

1 Elgin Street

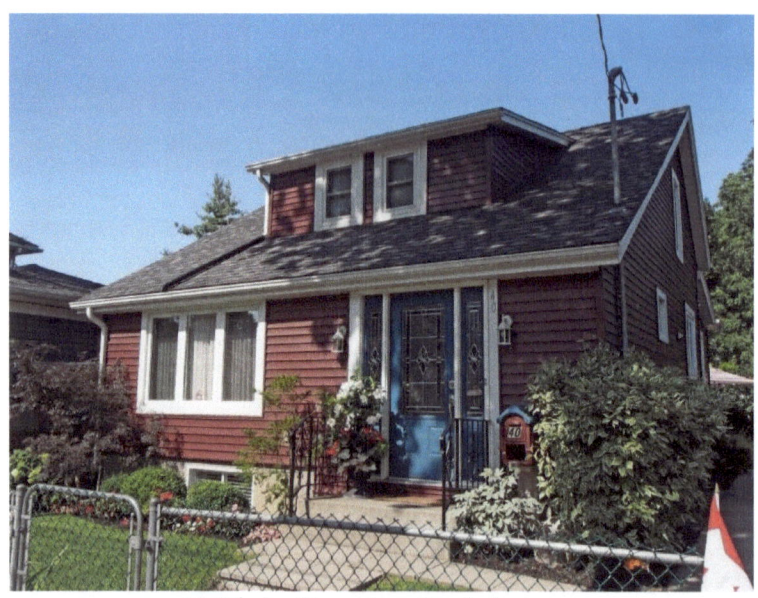

40 Elgin Street – shed dormer

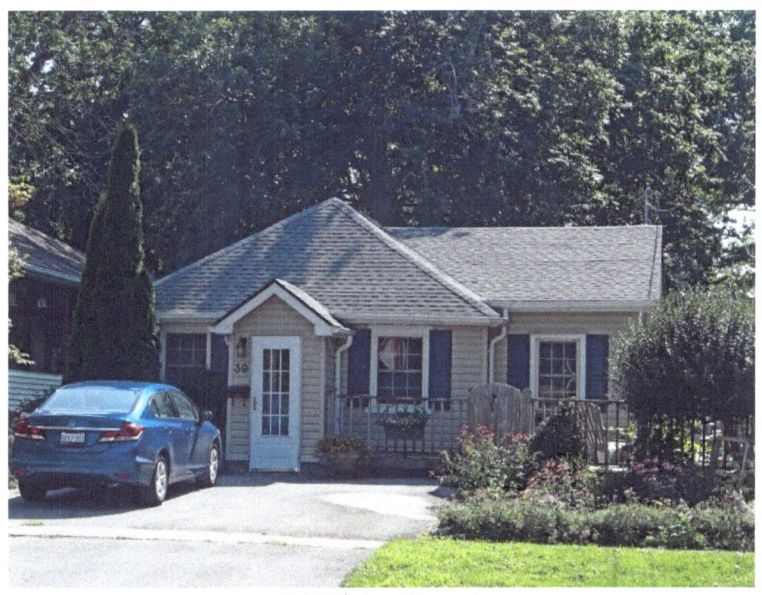

39 Elgin Street

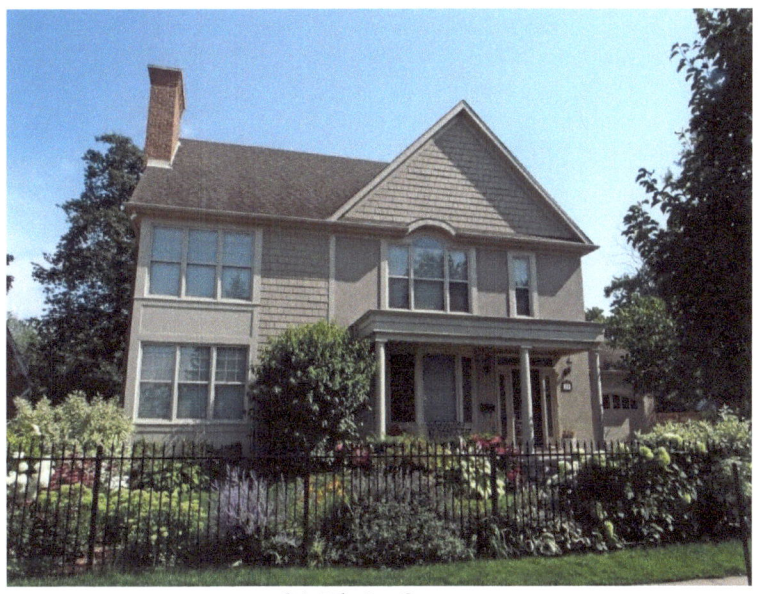

21 Elgin Street

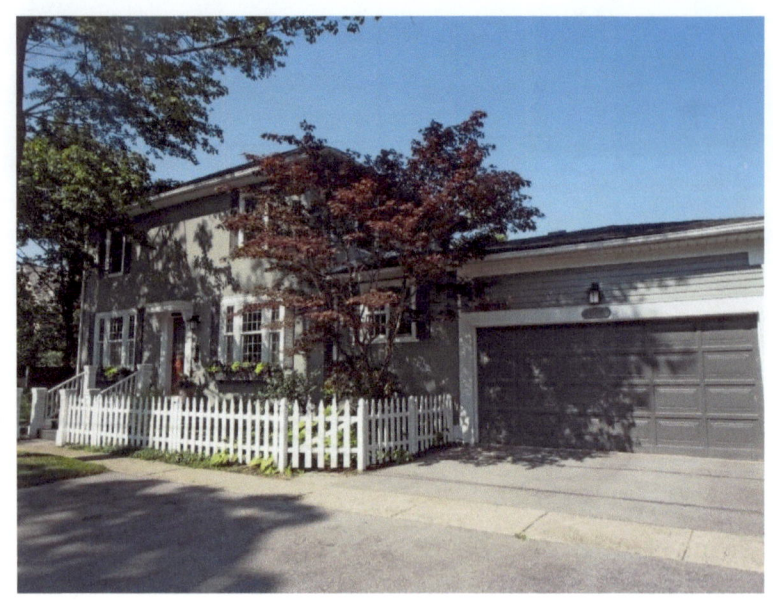

27 Elgin Street

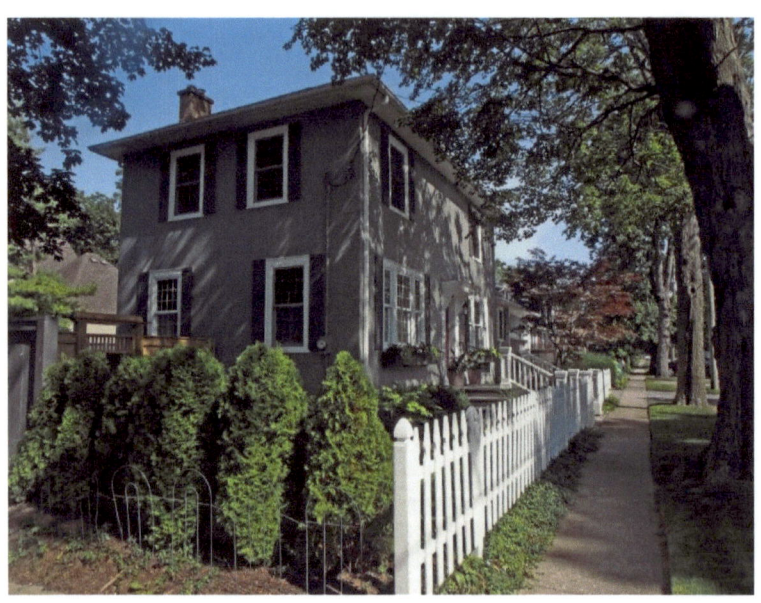

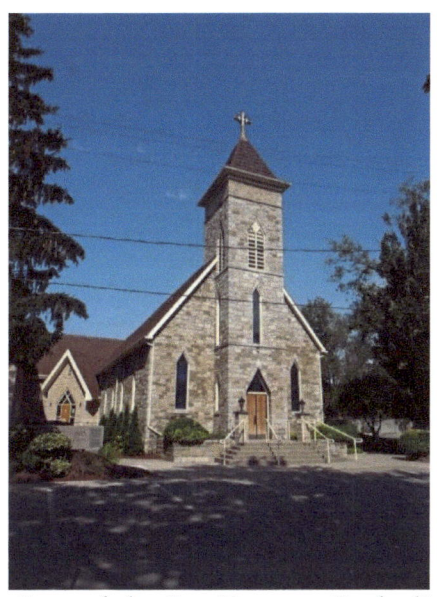

34 Elgin Street – Star of the Sea Roman Catholic Church – 1871 – Gothic, lancet windows, three-storey tower

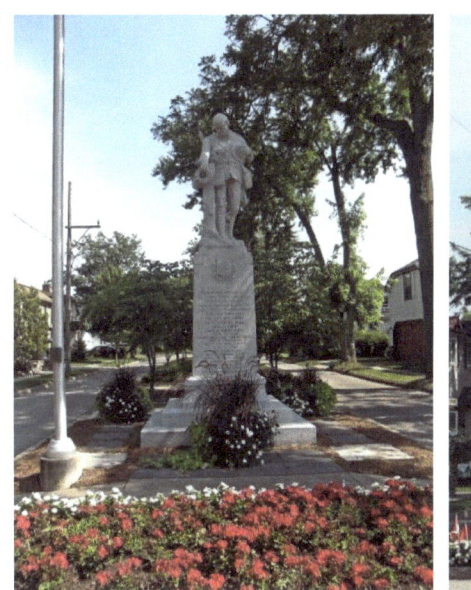 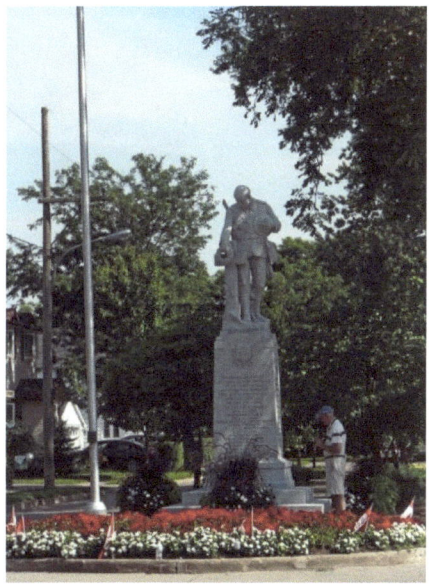

War Memorial for those who lost their lives in the two great wars

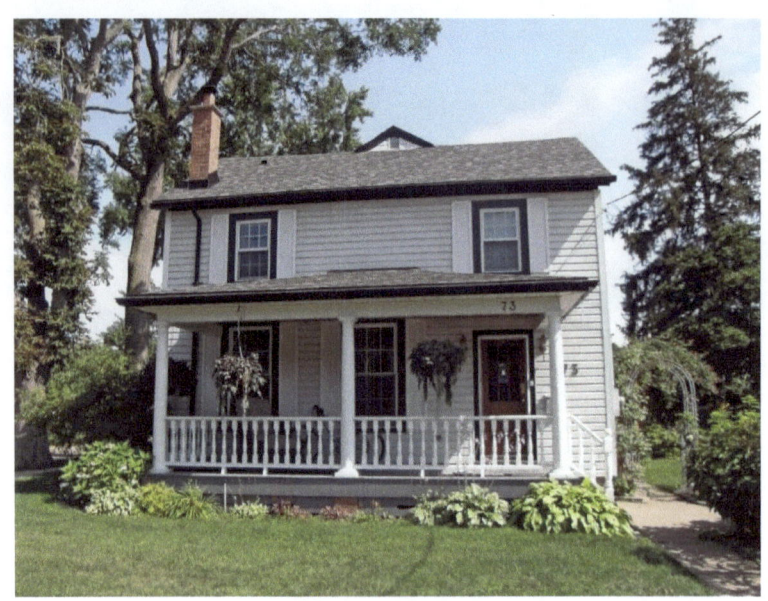

73 Ann Street

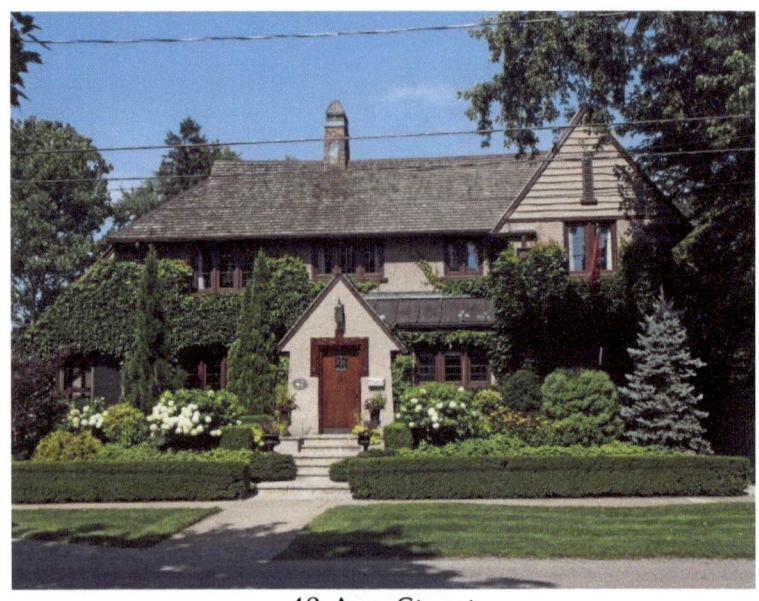

40 Ann Street

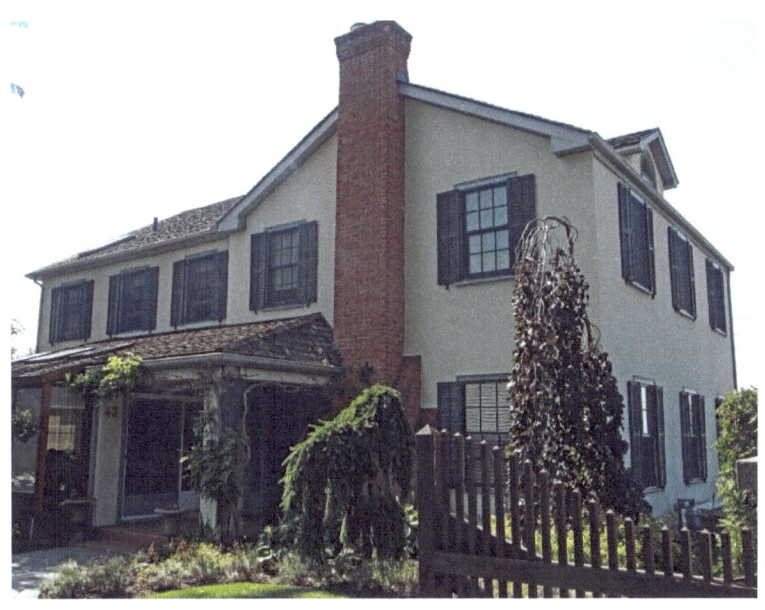

43 Ann Street

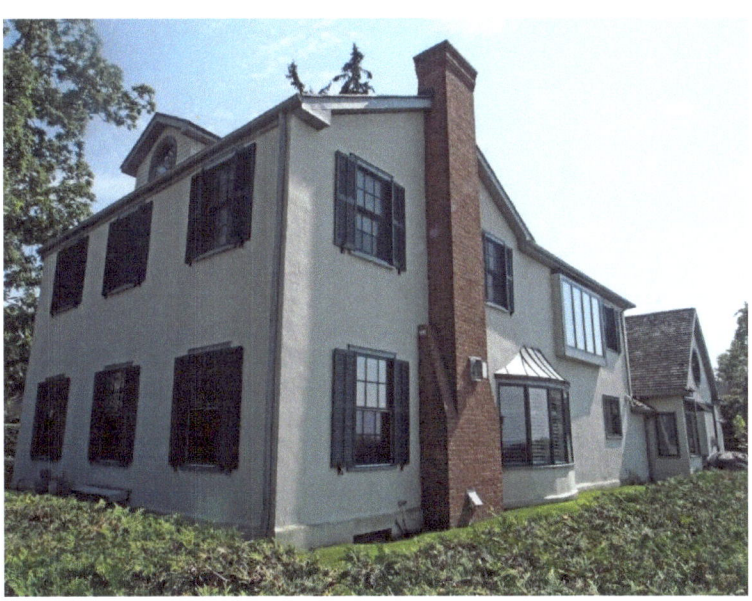

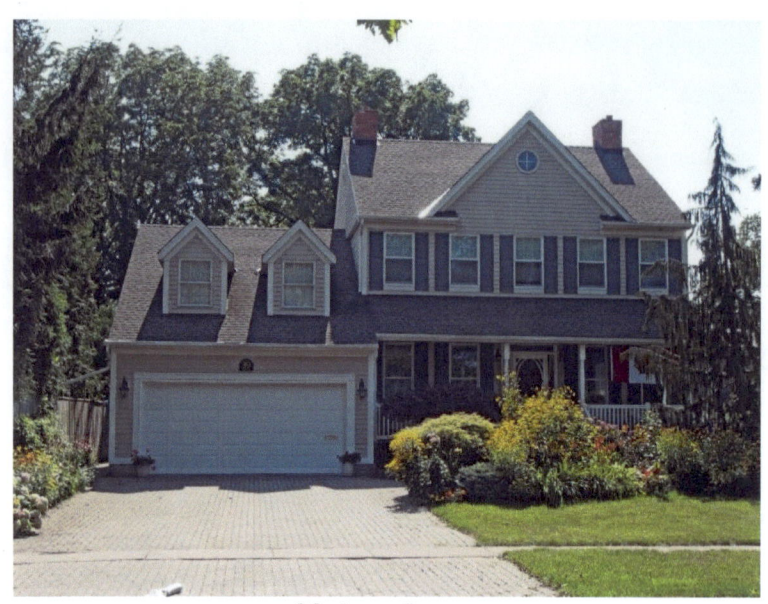

39 Ann Street

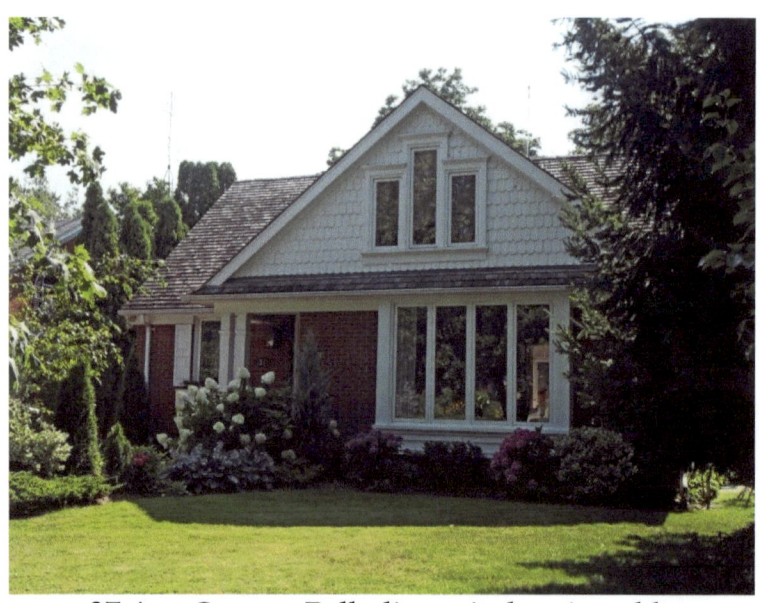

37 Ann Street – Palladian window in gable

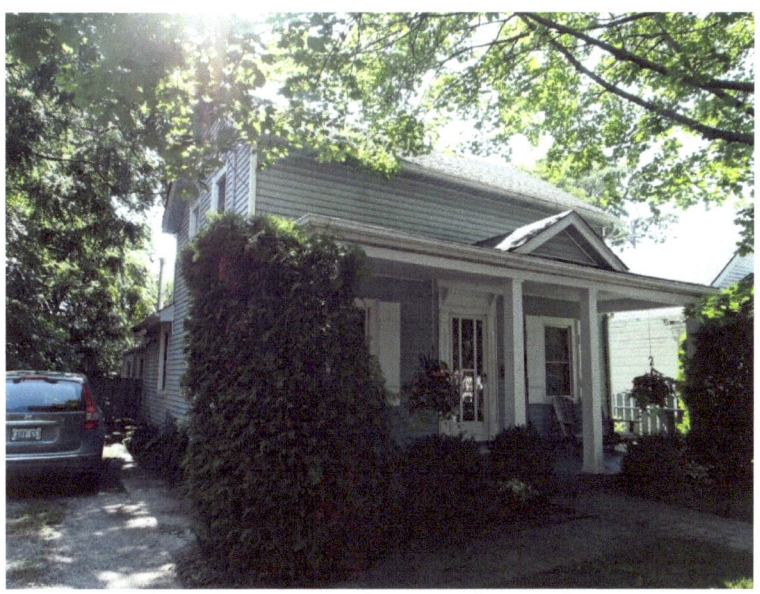

Ann Street – pediment above door

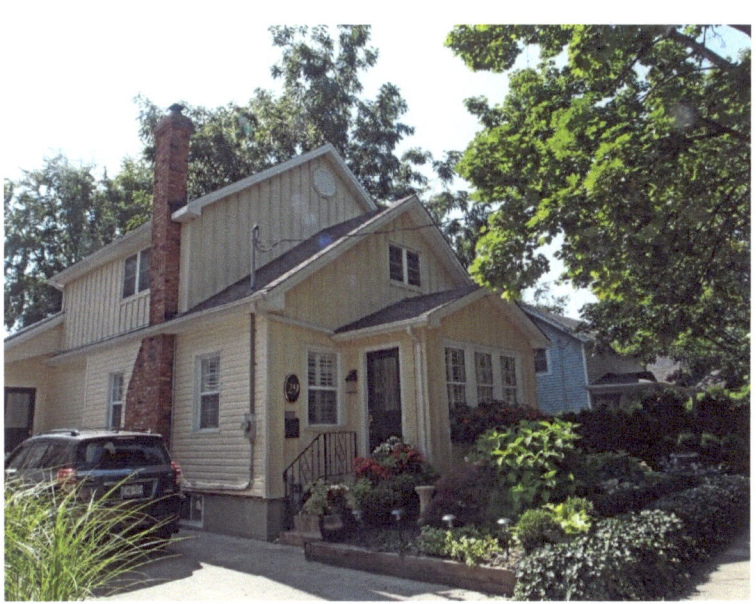

29 Ann Street

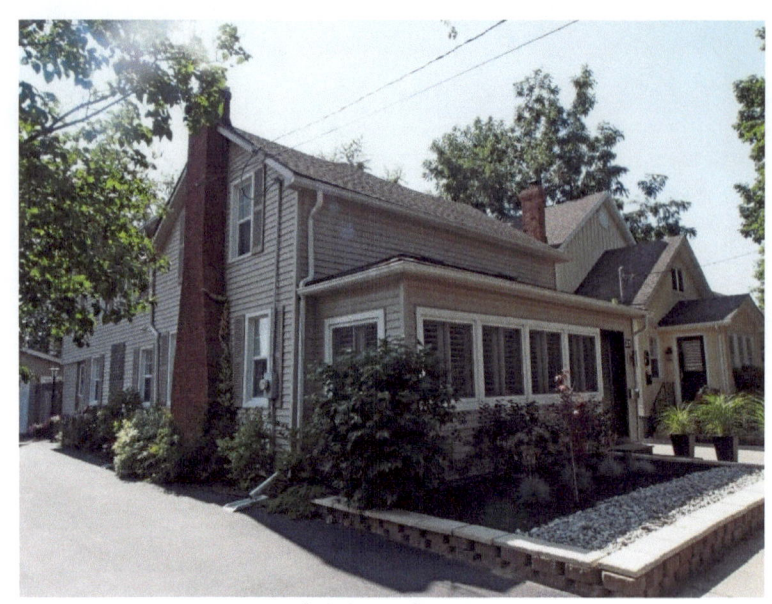

27 Ann Street

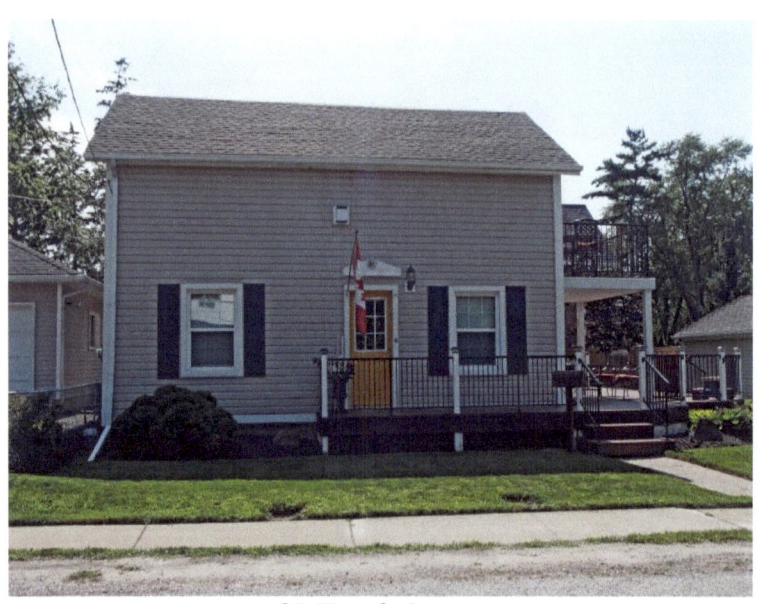

31 Brock Street

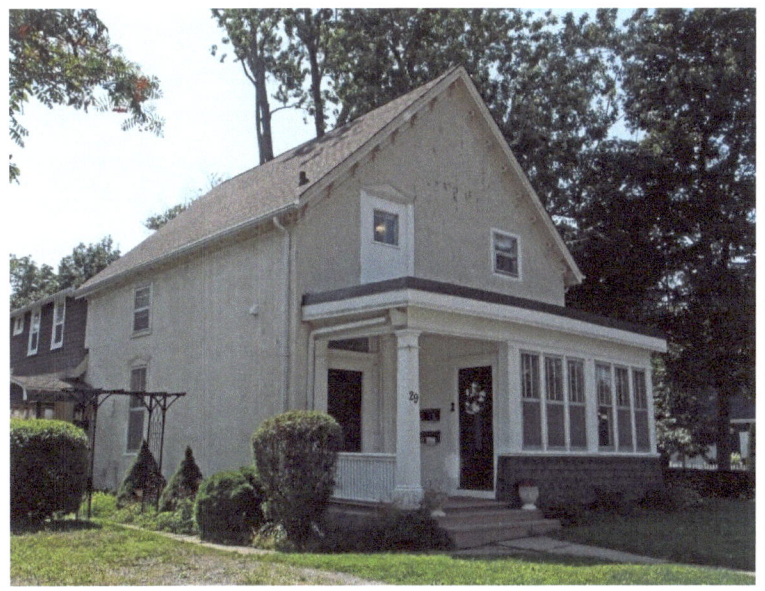

29 Brock Street

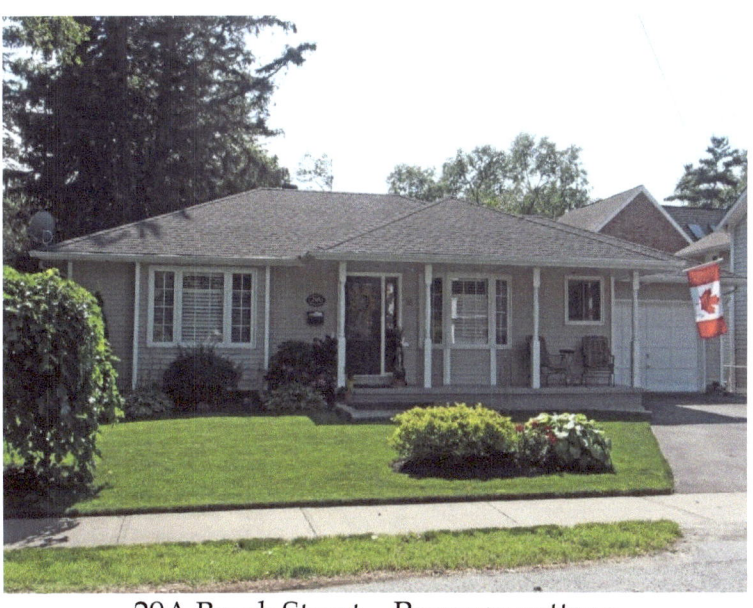

29A Brock Street – Regency cottage

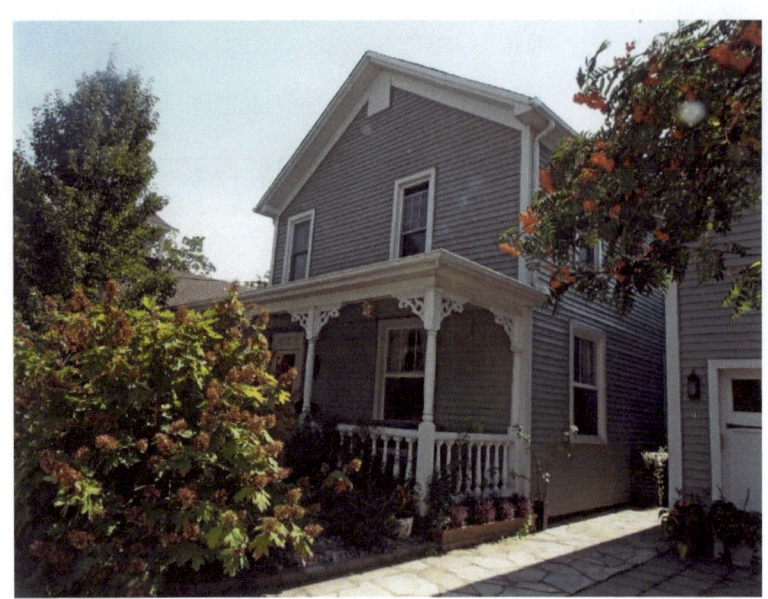

25 Brock Street – Gothic, bric-a-brac on veranda

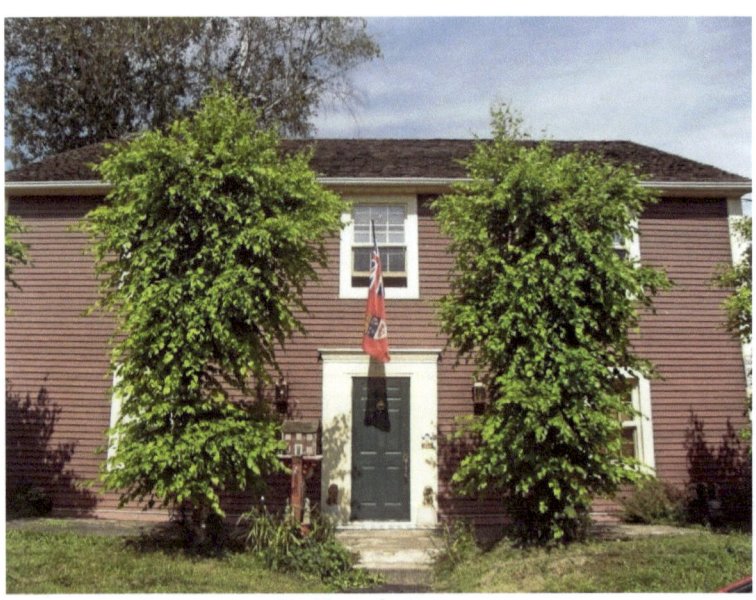

24 Brock Street

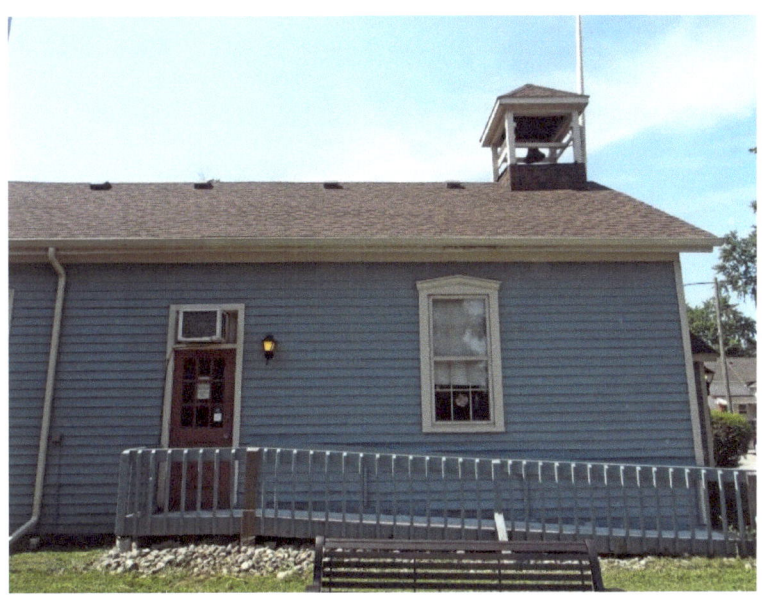

Brock Street – Port Dalhousie Town Hall

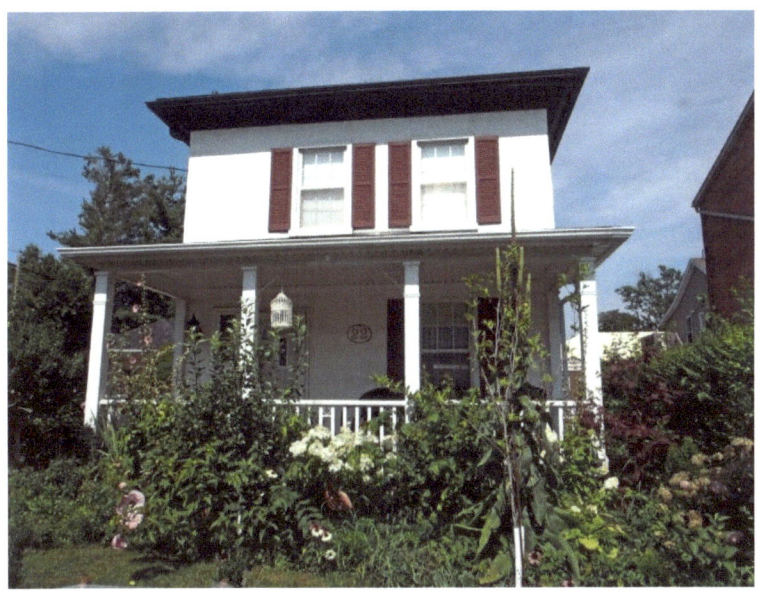

22 Brock Street

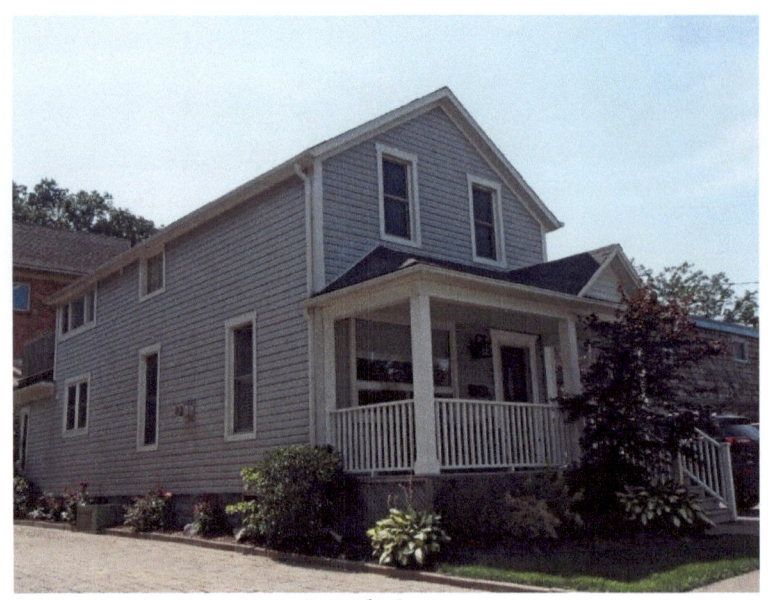

Brock Street

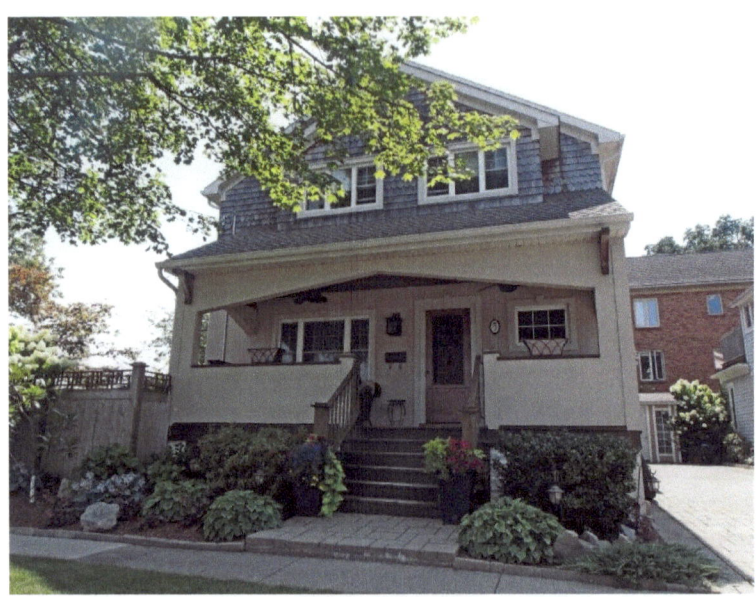

5 Brock Street

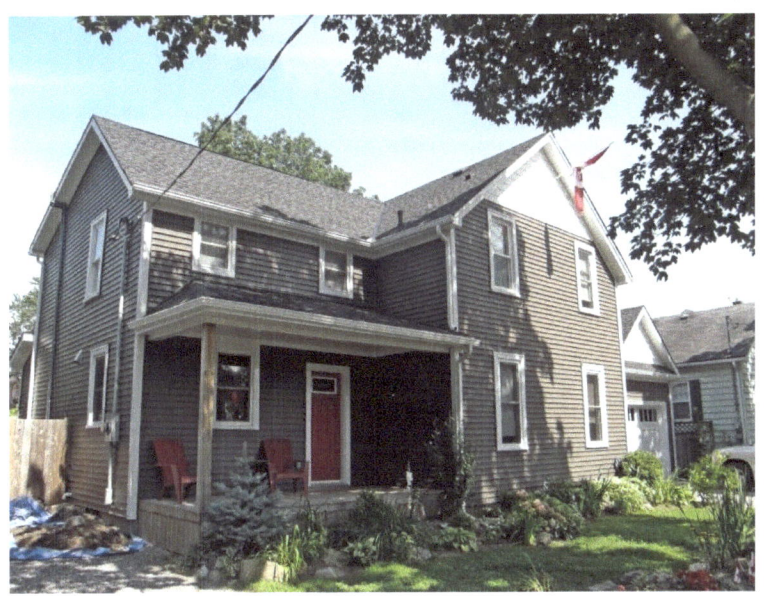

24 Simcoe Street

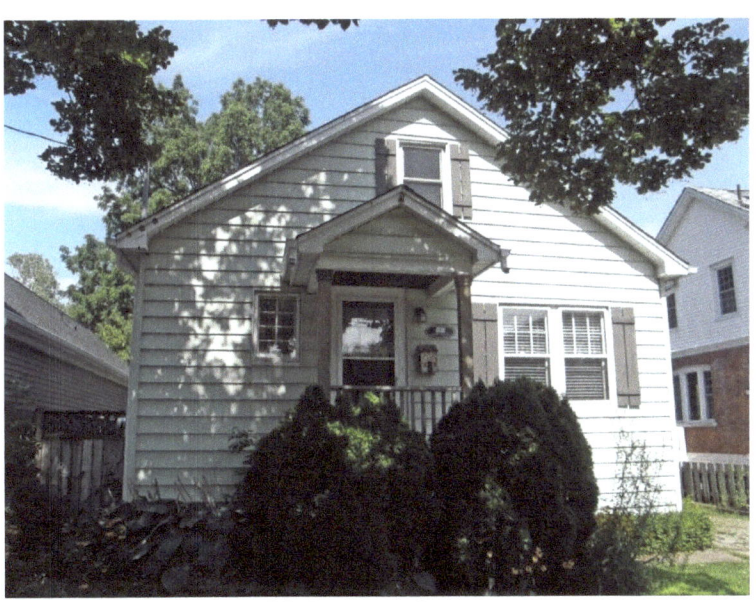

22 Simcoe Street

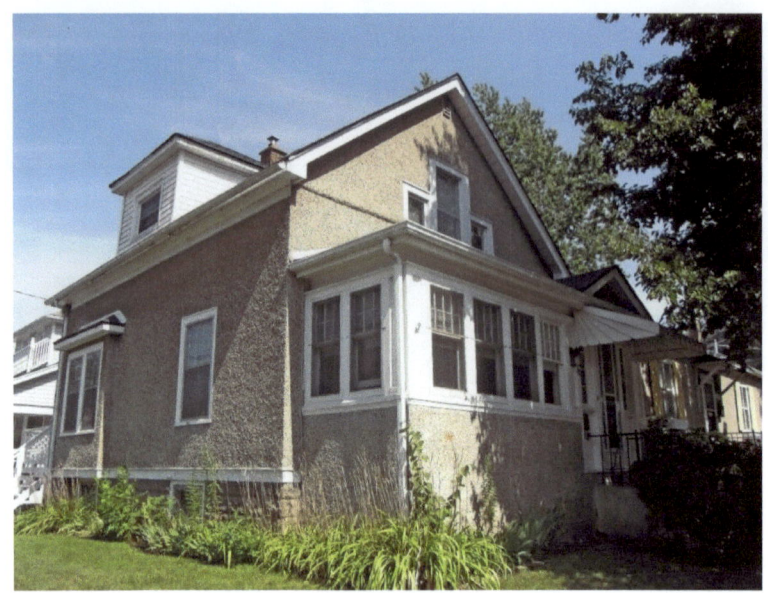

Palladian window in gable, pediment above entrance, dormer in attic

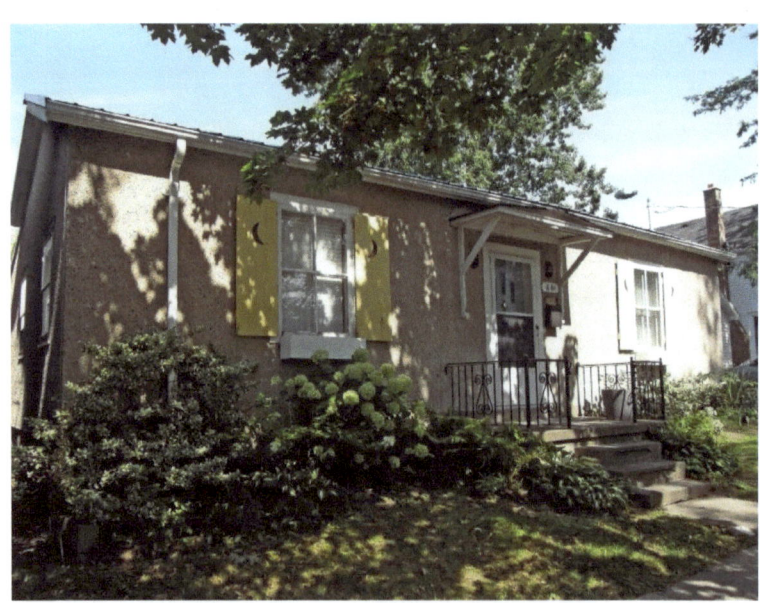

Simcoe Street – Regency cottage

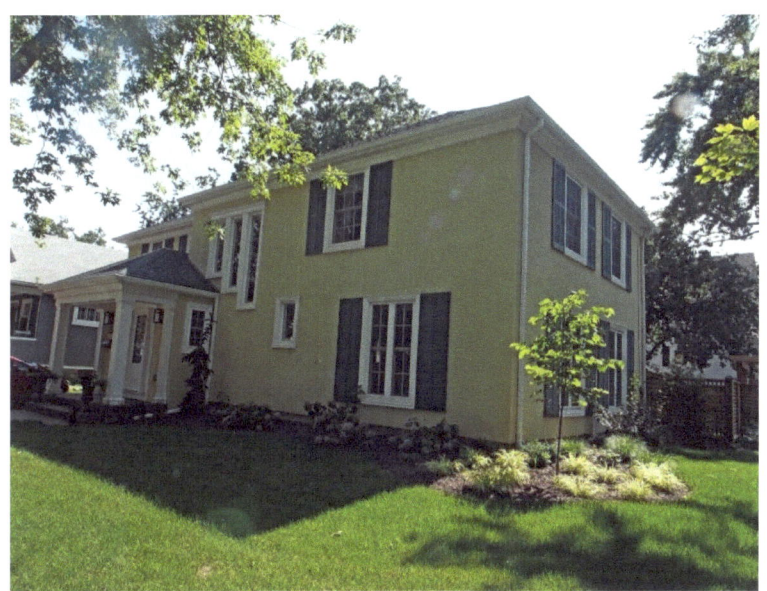

27 Simcoe Street

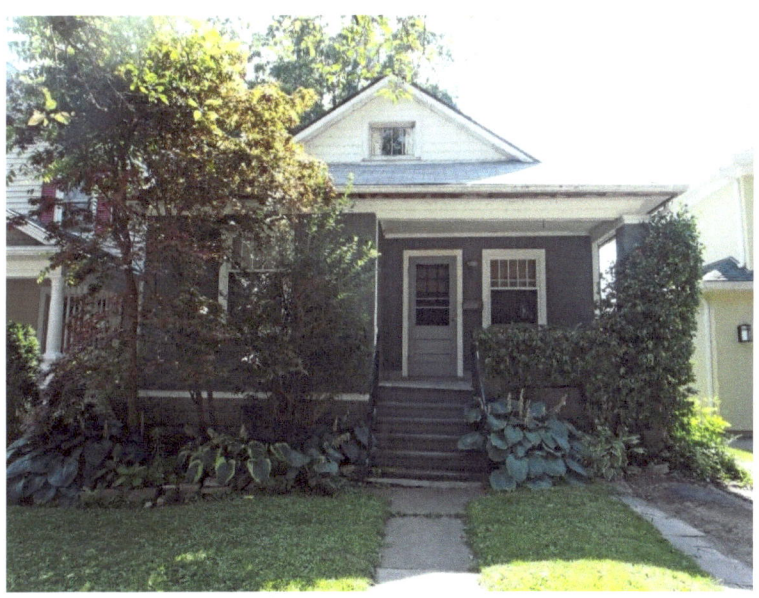

25 Simcoe Street

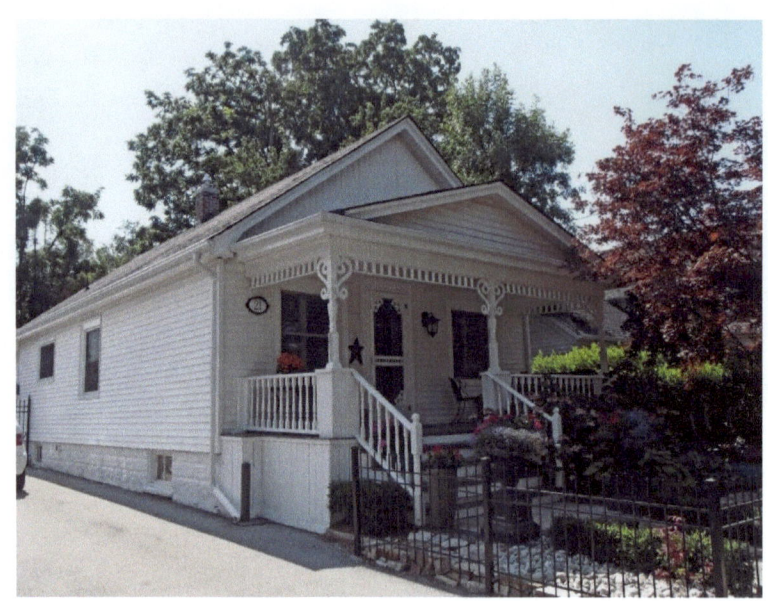

21 Simcoe Street – bric-a-brac on veranda

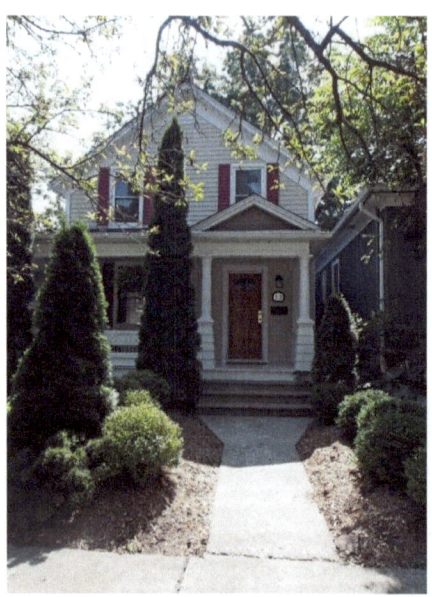

23 Simcoe Street - pediment

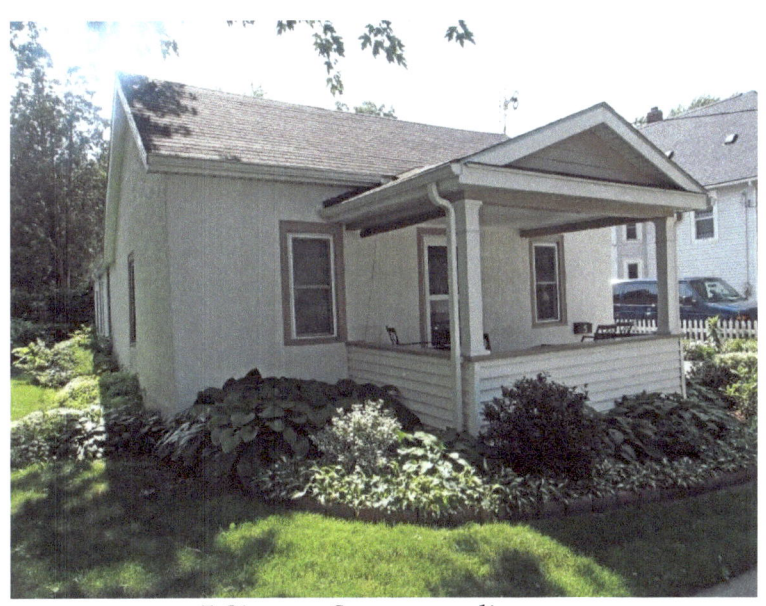

5 Simcoe Street - pediment

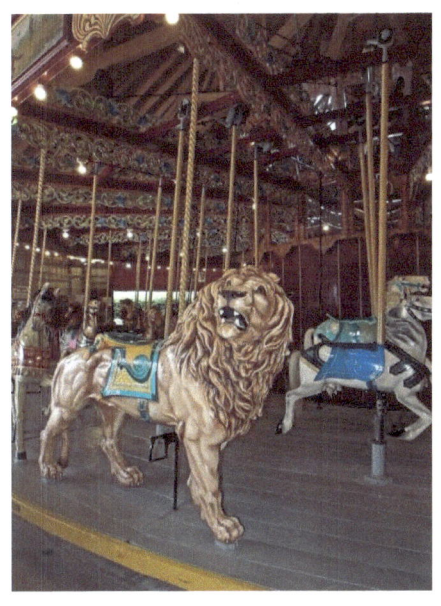

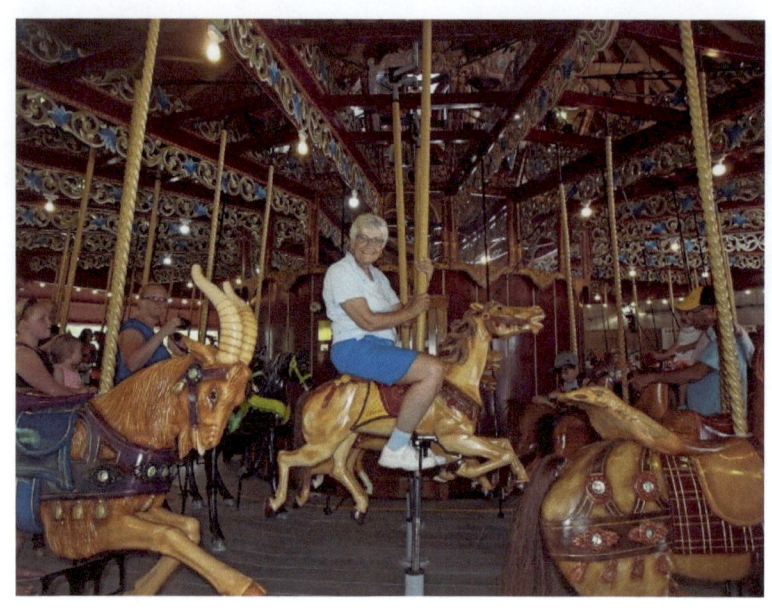

1 Lakeport Road – Lakeside Park Carousel

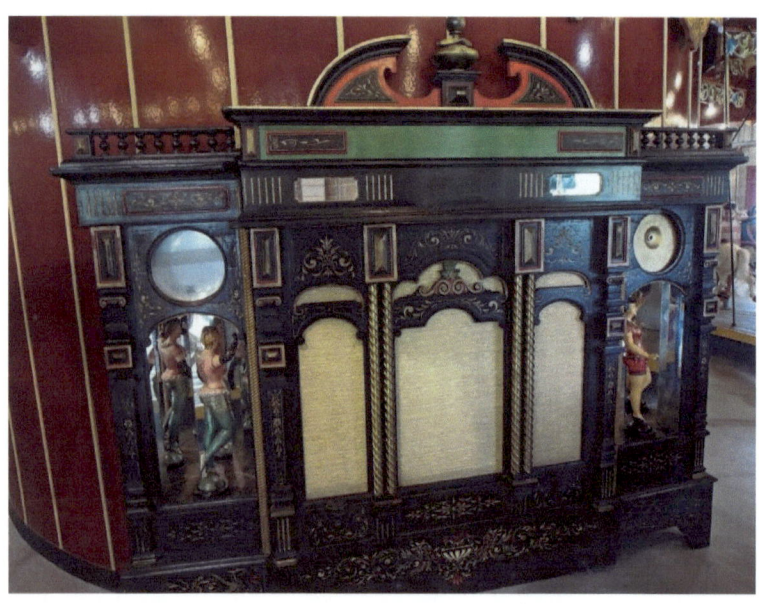

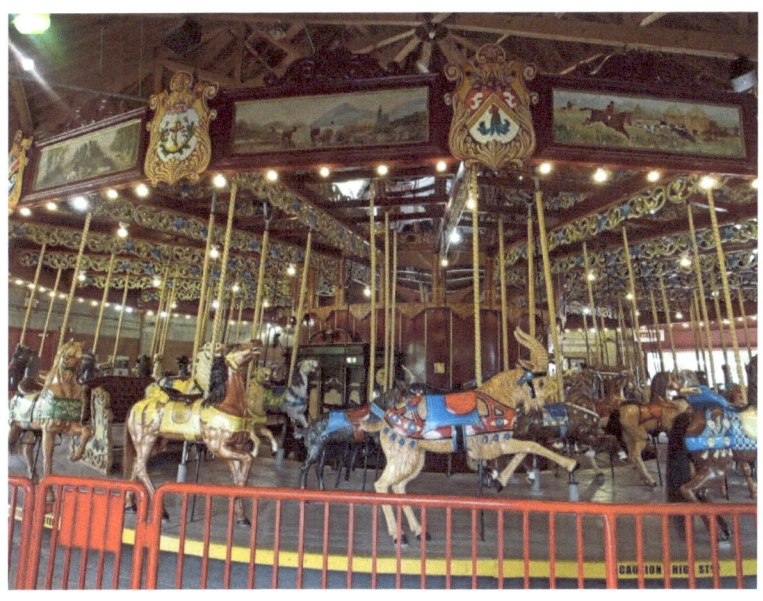

1 Lakeport Road – Lakeside Park Carousel

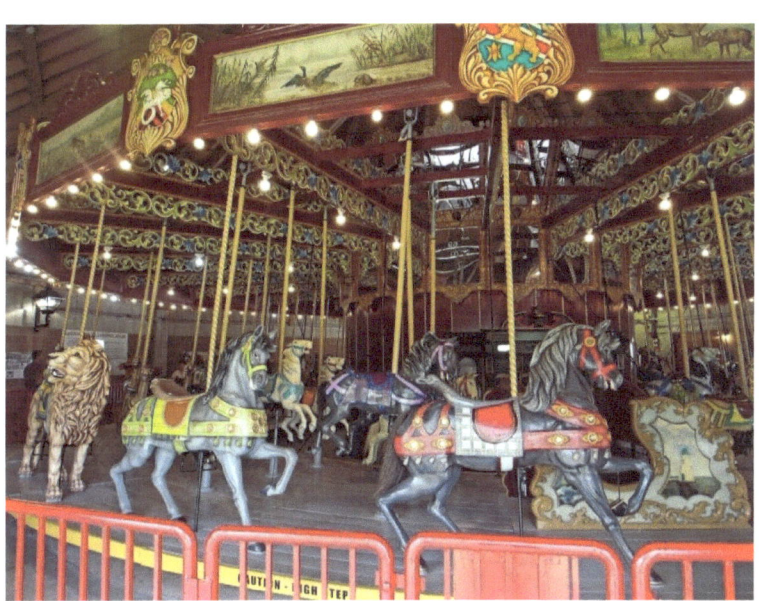

Architectural Terms

Bay Window: A window that projects out from a wall, in a semicircular, rectangular, or polygonal design. Used frequently in Gothic and Victorian designs. Example: 47 Dalhousie Avenue, Page 33	
Brackets: a decorative or weight-bearing structural element which forms a right angle with one side against a wall and the other under a projecting surface such as an eave or roof. Example: 29 Dalhousie Avenue, Page 40	
Dormer: (French for "sleep") a gable end window that pierces through the plane of a sloping roof surface to create usable space in the top floor or attic of a building by adding headroom. Example: 106 Dalhousie Avenue, Page 20	
Gable: the triangular portion of a wall between the edges of a sloping roof. Example: 147 Dalhousie Avenue, Page 12	
Gambrel Roof: a symmetrical two-sided roof with two slopes on each side; the upper slope is positioned at a shallow angle, while the lower slope is steep. It is similar to a mansard roof, but a gambrel has vertical gable ends instead of being hipped at the four corners of the building. Example: 94 Dalhousie Avenue, Page 21	
Hipped Roof: a roof where all sides slope downwards to the walls with no gables. Example: 36 Dalhousie Avenue, Page 36	

Lancet Window: a tall, narrow window with a pointed arch at its top. Example: 34 Elgin Street, Page 49	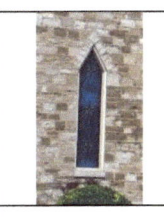
Palladian Window: a large window that is divided into three sections with the centre section larger than the two side sections and usually arched. Example: 76 Dalhousie Avenue, Page 24	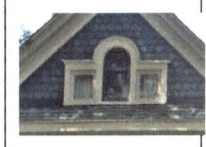
Pediment: a triangular section above the door or portico, usually supported by columns. The inside of the triangle is called the tympanum. Example: 23 Simcoe Street, Page 62	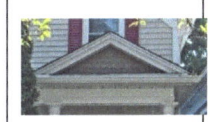
Quoin: masonry blocks at the corner of a wall, often a decorative feature, usually larger or of a different colour than the rest of the wall. Example: 82 Dalhousie Avenue, Page 23	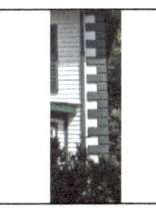
Sidelight: a vertical window that flanks a door, and is often used to emphasize the importance of a primary entrance. **Transom Window:** the light above the doorway, also called a fanlight. Example: Dalhousie Avenue, Page 39	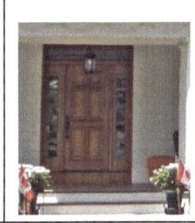
Verge board and Finial: also called bargeboards – hang from the projecting end of a roof and are often elaborately carved and ornamented. **Finial:** ornament added to the top of a gable, pinnacle, canopy or spire – a Gothic element. Example: 127 Dalhousie Avenue, Page 17	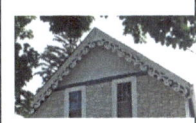

Building Styles

Gothic Revival, 1830-1890 – These decorative buildings have sharply-pitched gables with highly detailed verge boards, pointed-arch window openings, and dichromatic brickwork. It is a common style in Ontario. Example: 29 Dalhousie Avenue, Page 40	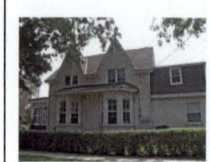
Neo-Classical, 1810-1850 – Many Upper Canadians returning from the War of 1812 with the United States were Loyalists who had inherited land and means from their forefathers. Once the conflict had passed, they had the money and the time to expand their holdings and indulge their architectural whims. The buildings were constructed on the traditional Georgian plan, but with a new gaiety and light-heartedness. Detailing became more refined, delicate, and elegant. Example: 52 Dalhousie Avenue, Page 31	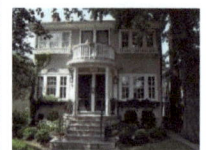
Neo-colonial (also Colonial Revival, Georgian Revival or Neo-Georgian) – Architecture from the 18th and early 19th centuries in Ontario includes a wide assortment of detailing and ornament applied to a design centered around the fireplace and the source of water. Structures are typically two stories, have a symmetrical front facade with elaborate front doorways, often with decorative crown pediments, fanlights, and sidelights, symmetrical windows flanking the front entrance, often in pairs or threes, and columned porches. Example: 22 Dalhousie Avenue, Page 43	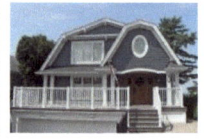

Regency Cottage, 1830-1860 – This style originated in England in 1815 and spread to Ontario later in the 19th century as British officers retired to Canada. It is a modest one-storey house with a low-pitched hip roof and has a symmetrical front façade. Example: 158 Dalhousie Avenue, Page 10	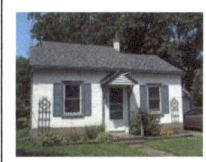
Saltbox: A saltbox is a building with a long, pitched roof that slopes down to the back, generally a wooden frame house. A saltbox has just one storey in the back and two stories in the front. The asymmetry of the unequal sides and the long, low rear roof line are the most distinctive features of a saltbox, which takes its name from its resemblance to a wooden lidded box in which salt was once kept. The earliest saltbox houses were created when a lean-to addition was added onto the rear of the original house extending the roof line sometimes to less than six feet from ground level. Example: 153 Dalhousie Avenue, Page 11	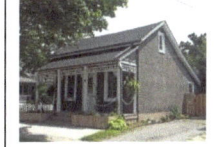